Appala⟨ to

Maryland and Northern Virginia
With Side Trails

2015
Eighteenth Edition

The Potomac Appalachian Trail Club
118 Park Street, SE
Vienna, Virginia 22180
www.patc.net

APPALACHIAN TRAIL GUIDE
TO
MARYLAND AND
NORTHERN VIRGINIA

2015
Eighteenth Edition edited by
John Hedrick

Copyright ©2015 by the Potomac Appalachian Trail Club
118 Park St., SE
Vienna, VA 22180-4609

Library of Congress Control Number: 2015932120
ISBN 978-0-915746-60-6

Abbreviations

AT or Trail	Appalachian Trail
ATC or Conservancy	Appalachian Trail Conservancy
mi	mile or miles
PATC	Potomac Appalachian Trail Club
USGS	U.S. Geological Survey
yd	yard or yards

Acknowledgments

This edition has been made possible with the help of many volunteers, including Jon Rindt, Chris Brunton, Rick Canter, Emeline Otey, Alan Kahan, Dave Pierce, and numerous other club members.

Cover photo: View from Jefferson Rock by Aaron Watkins

The Potomac Appalachian Trail Club expressly denies any liability for any accident or injury to persons using these trails. Hikers should be aware of various hazards on the trails.

Water purity along trails cannot be guaranteed. All water from natural sources, including springs, should be treated before use.

Acadia's Waterfall   Laurie Pottegier

CONTENTS

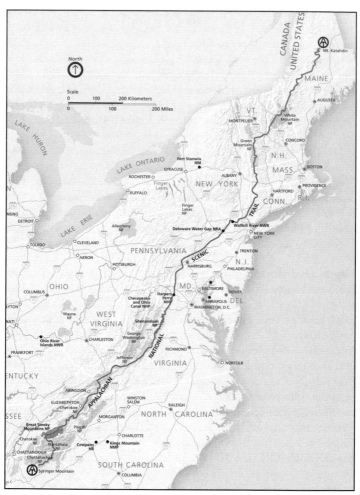

Appalachian Trail Map   Courtesy of National Park Service

ABOUT THE APPALACHIAN TRAIL

Welcome to America's best-known long-distance footpath, the Appalachian Trail. If you've never visited it before, you're in for a memorable time, and we hope this official guidebook will help you make the most of it. If you know the Trail, but not this part of it, we hope this book will help you discover new aspects of an experience that changes from state to state, mile to mile, and season to season.

Not long after the end of World War I, a Massachusetts forester and dreamer named Benton MacKaye envisioned a footpath running along the crests of the eastern mountains, from New England to the southern Appalachians. The work of thousands of volunteers helped that dream become the Appalachian Trail, which, as of 2015, extends 2,189 miles between Mount Katahdin, in central Maine, and Springer Mountain, in northern Georgia. Its terrain ranges from swampland bog bridges to near-vertical rock scrambles that challenge the fittest wilderness trekker; its white "blazes" lead from busy small-town streets to remote mountain ridges, days from the nearest road crossing.

The "*AT*," as it's called by hikers, is a linear trail that can be enjoyed in small pieces or large chunks. Hikers follow its blazes on round-trip day-hikes, on loop-hikes (where side-trails connect with it and form a loop), on one-way "section-hikes" or overnight backpacking trips that cover short or long segments, or on end-to-end "thru-hikes" that cover the entire Trail. It is continuously marked, using a standard system of paint blazes and signs, and is cleared of undergrowth and maintained to permit single-file hiking. (Bicycles, horses, and motorized vehicles are not permitted along most of the route.) Many campsites and more than 250 primitive woodland shelters are located along the Trail, typically about a day's hike apart. The path itself is usually dirt, rock or grass, and only very short segments are paved or wheelchair accessible.

This remarkable footpath is much more than just a walk through the woods. When it was first begun in the 1920s and completed in the 1930s, it was little known and rarely traveled. Large parts of it were on private property. Since 1968, it has been a part of the same national park system that includes Yellowstone, Yosemite, and the Great Smoky Mountains. Its official name today is the Appalachian National Scenic Trail, and 99.9 percent of it runs over public lands. Hundreds of roads cross it, and hundreds of side trails intersect with it. In some parts, the Trail "corridor" is only a few hundred feet wide; in other parts, entire mountains are protected by it.

Unlike other well-known national parks, there's no "main entrance" to the *AT*, with a gate and a ranger collecting tickets. You can begin or end your hike at hundreds of places between its northern and southern ends. As the longest, skinniest part of America's national park system, the *AT* stretches across 14 different states and passes through more than 60 federal, state, and local parks and forests. Maybe the most important difference between the *AT* and other national-park units is that it was built by volunteers, and volunteers still are responsible for maintaining it. The *AT* relies on a system known as "cooperative management" rather than on a large, paid federal staff. Yes, there is a handful of National Park Service staff members and a ranger assigned to the Appalachian National Scenic Trail Park Office in Harpers Ferry, West Virginia, but thousands of the people who maintain, patrol, and monitor the footpath and its surrounding lands are outdoor lovers like you. Each year, as members of 31 "maintaining clubs" up and down the Appalachians, they volunteer hundreds of thousands of hours of their time looking after this public treasure. They would welcome your help.

The Appalachian Trail Conservancy

The Appalachian Trail Conservancy (ATC) is the volunteer-based organization that teaches people about the Trail, coordinates the work of the maintaining clubs, and works with the government agencies, individuals, and companies that own the land that the Trail passes over. The membership of the ATC includes more than 40,000 hikers and Trail enthusiasts. Members' dues and contributions help support a paid staff at the ATC headquarters in Harpers Ferry and at field offices in New Hampshire, Pennsylvania, Virginia, and North Carolina. Their World Wide Web site, www.appalachiantrail.org, is a good source of information about the Trail.

TIPS FOR ENJOYING THE APPALACHIAN TRAIL

Follow the Blazes

The Appalachian Trail is marked for daylight travel in both directions, using a system of paint "blazes" on trees, posts, and rocks. There are some local variations, but most hikers grasp the system quickly. Above treeline, and where snow or fog may obscure paint marks, posts and rock piles called "cairns" are used to identify the route.

A blaze is a rectangle of paint in a prominent place along a trail. White paint blazes two inches wide and six inches high mark the *AT* itself. Side trails and shelter trails use blue blazes; blazes of other colors and shapes mark intersecting trails. Two white blazes, one above the other, signal an obscure turn, route change, incoming side trail, or other situation that requires you to be especially alert. In some states, one of the two blazes will be offset in the direction of the turn.

If you have gone a quarter-mile without seeing a blaze, stop. Retrace your steps until you locate a blaze. Then, check to ensure that you haven't missed a turn. Often a glance backward will reveal blazes meant for hikers traveling in the opposite direction. Volunteer Trail maintainers regularly relocate small sections of the path around hazards, undesirable features, or off private property. When your map or guidebook indicates one route, and the blazes show another, follow the blazes.

Leave No Trace

As more and more people use the Trail and other backcountry areas, it becomes more important to learn to enjoy wild places without ruining them. The best way to do this is to understand and practice the principles of Leave No Trace, a seven-point ethic for enjoying the backcountry that applies to everything from a picnic outing to a long-distance expedition.

Leave No Trace is also a non-profit organization dedicated to teaching the principles of low-impact use. For more information, contact Leave No Trace at www.lnt.org, or call (800) 332-4100.

The seven principles of the Leave No Trace ethic are:

1. Plan ahead and prepare. Evaluate the risks associated with your outing, identify campsites and destinations in advance, use maps and guides, and be ready for bad weather. When people don't plan ahead, they're more likely to damage the backcountry.

2. Travel and camp on durable surfaces. Stay on trails and don't take short-cuts across switchbacks or other bends in the path. Keep off fragile trailside areas, such as bogs or alpine zones. Camp in designated spots, such as shelters and existing campsites, so that unspoiled areas aren't trampled and denuded.

3. Dispose of waste properly. Bury or pack out excrement, including pet droppings. Pack out all trash and food waste, including that left behind by others. Don't bury trash or food, and don't try to burn packaging materials in campfires.

4. Leave what you find. Don't take flowers or other sensitive natural resources. Don't disturb artifacts such as native American arrowheads or the stone walls and cellar holes of historical woodland homesteads.

5. Minimize campfire impacts. Campfires are enjoyable, but they also create the worst visual and ecological impact of any backcountry camping practice. If possible, cook on a backpacking stove instead of a fire. Where fires are permitted, build them only in established fire rings, and don't add rocks to an existing ring. Keep fires small. Burn only dead and downed wood that can be broken by hand—leave axes and saws at home. Never leave your campfire unattended, and drown it when you leave.

6. Respect wildlife. Don't feed or disturb wildlife. Store food properly to avoid attracting bears, varmints, and rodents. If you bring a pet, keep it leashed.

7. Be considerate of other visitors. Limit overnight groups to ten or fewer, twenty-five on day trips. Minimize noise and intrusive behavior. Share shelters and other facilities. Be considerate of Trail neighbors.

A Few Cautions

The *AT* is a scenic trail through the forests of the Appalachian Mountains. It is full of natural splendors and is fun to hike. Some of the Trail is very steep and runs deep in the woods, along the crests of rocky mountain ridges, miles from the nearest houses or paved roads. It will test your physical conditioning and skills. Plan your hike, and prepare sensibly.

Before you set out to hike the Trail, take a few minutes to review the information in this guidebook. It is as current as possible, but conditions and footpath locations sometimes change between guidebook editions. On the Trail, please pay close attention to—and follow—the blazes and any directional signs that mark the route, even if the book describes a different route.

Many good books are available in your local bookstore and library. If you've never hiked before, we recommend that you take the time to read one or two and to research equipment, camping techniques, and trip planning. If your only hiking and camping experience is in local parks and forests, be aware that hiking and camping in the mountains can be extremely strenuous and disorienting and has its own particular challenges. You will sometimes encounter wildlife and will have to make do with primitive (or nonexistent) sanitary facilities. Remember that water in the backcountry, even at water sources mentioned in this guidebook, needs to be treated for microorganisms before you drink it.

Responsibility for Safety

Know that you are responsible for your own safety, for the safety of those with you, and for making sure that your food and water are safe for consumption. Hiking the *AT* is no more dangerous than many other popular outdoor activities, but, although the Trail is part of the national park system, it is not the proverbial "walk in the park." The Appalachian Trail Conservancy and its member maintaining clubs cannot ensure the safety of any hiker on the Trail; as a hiker, you assume the risk for any accident, illness, or injury that might occur there.

The Appalachian Trail is safer than most places, but a few crimes of violence have occurred. Awareness is one of your best lines of defense. Be aware of what you are doing, where you are, and to whom you are talking. Hikers looking out for each other can be an effective "community watch." Be prudent and cautious without allowing common sense to slip into paranoia. Remember to trust your gut—it's usually right. Other tips include the following:

- Don't hike alone. If you are by yourself and encounter a stranger who makes you feel uncomfortable, say you are with a group that is behind you. Be creative. If in doubt, move on. Even a partner is no guarantee of safety, however. Pay attention to your instincts about other people.

- Leave your hiking itinerary and timetable with someone at home. Be sure your contacts and your family know your "Trail name," if you use one. Check in regularly, and establish a procedure to follow if you fail to check in. On short hikes, provide your contacts with the numbers of the land-managing agencies for the area of your hike, and your expected time of return. On extended hikes, provide ATC's number, (304-535-6331).

- Be wary of strangers. Be friendly, but cautious. Don't tell strangers your plans. Avoid people who act suspiciously, seem hostile, or are intoxicated.

- Don't camp near roads.

- Dress conservatively to avoid unwanted attention.

- Eliminate opportunities for theft. Don't bring jewelry. Hide your money. If you leave your pack, hide it, or leave it with someone trustworthy. Don't leave valuables or equipment, (especially in sight) in vehicles parked at Trailheads.

- Use the Trail registers (the notebooks stored at most shelters). Sign in, leave a note, and report any suspicious activities. If someone needs to locate you, or if a serious crime has been committed along the Trail, the first place authorities will look is in the registers.

- Report any crime or harassment to the local authorities and the ATC.

Path along the trail   Darrell Midgette

USE OF THE GUIDE AND TRAIL

Disclaimer Notice to All Trail Users and Landowners

Although the editor, the PATC, and ATC strive for accuracy and thoroughness in the materials published, it is impossible to ensure that all the information accurately describes the condition and location of the Trail. Consequently, the editor, the PATC and its agents, and the ATC expressly disclaim any liability for inaccuracies in this book. The Trail crosses both private and public lands, the owners or administrators of which may alter Trail conditions and impose regulations on the use of the Trail. The editor, the PATC and its agents, and the ATC expressly disclaim any liability for the negligence, wrongful actions or omissions of any landowner with respect to the Trail, and of any Trail users with respect to private or public property.

This Guide and associated maps refer to springs as sources of water. The purity of water from any sources cannot be guaranteed, and the editor, the PATC and its agents, and the ATC expressly disclaim liability for any impurities in such water. Extreme care must be used in drinking such water. All water should be purified by boiling, or chemically treated before use, but even these measures will not guarantee the safe use of such water, particularly if the water is chemically polluted. Creeks, rivers, ponds, and lakes should never be used as a water source. The editor, the PATC and its agents, and the ATC expressly disclaim any liability for the condition of the Trail and for all occurrences on the Trail.

THE GUIDEBOOK

Rather than trying to keep track of several hundred miles of the Trail from beginning to end, the Trail's maintainers break it down into smaller "sections." Each section typically covers the area between important road crossings or natural features and can vary from three to 30 miles in length. A typical section is from five to 15 miles long. This guidebook is organized according to those sections, beginning with the northernmost in the coverage area and ending with the southernmost. Each section makes up a chapter.

Brief description of section

Each chapter begins with a brief description of the route. The description mentions highlights and prominent features and gives a sense of what it's like to hike the section as a whole.

Road access

Directions are given for driving to northern and southern trailheads.

Section map and profile

At the beginning of the each section description, appropriate maps will be indicated along with a schematic profile of the high and low points in the section. A schematic profile of the high and low points in the section gives you an idea of how much climbing or descending is ahead.

Shelters, campsites and other public facilities

Each chapter also includes an overview of shelters and campsites for the section, including the distance between shelters and information about water supplies. Along some parts of the Trail, particularly north of the Mason-Dixon Line, the designated sites are the only areas in which camping is permitted. In other parts of the Trail, even where "dispersed camping" is allowed, we recommend that hikers "Leave No Trace" and reduce their impact on the Trail's resources by using established campsites. If camping is restricted in a section, it will be noted here.

Supplies

Locations of nearby towns, stores, and restaurants are described where the Trail crosses a road. Shelters and available water sources in the section are noted.

Trail description

Trail descriptions appear on the right-hand pages of each chapter. Although the description reads from north to south, it is organized for both northbound and southbound hikers. Northbound hikers should start at the end of the chapter and read up, using the mileages in the right-hand column. Southbound hikers should read down, using the mileages in the left-hand column. The description includes obvious landmarks you will pass, though it may not include all stream crossings, summits, or side-trails. Where the Trail route becomes confusing, the guide will provide both north- and southbound directions from the landmark. When a feature appears in bold type, it means that you should see the section highlights for more detail.

Section highlights

On the left-hand pages of each chapter, you will find cultural, historical, natural, and practical information about the bold items in the Trail description. That includes detailed information about Trailheads, shelters, and campsites, along with notes on the historical and cultural resources of the route, notes on landforms and natural history, and descriptions of side trails.

GUIDEBOOK CONVENTIONS

North or "Compass-north"?

For the sake of convenience, the directions north, south, east and west in the guide refer to the general north–south orientation of the Trail, rather than the true north or magnetic north of maps and charts. In other words, when a hiker is northbound on the Trail, whatever is to his left will be referred to as "west" and whatever is to the right will be "east." For southbounders, the opposite is true.

Although this is instinctively the way *AT* hikers orient themselves, it can be slightly confusing for the first-time *AT* hiker, since the Trail does not always follow an actual north–south orientation. For example, you might be "northbound" along the Trail (headed toward Maine), but, because of a sharp turn or a switchback up the side of a mountain, your compass will tell you you're actually pointed south for a while. Nevertheless, in this guide, a trail or road intersecting on the left side of the *AT* for the northbound hiker will always be referred to as "intersecting on the west side of the *AT*," even where the compass says otherwise.

When the compass direction of an object is important, as when directing attention to a certain feature seen from a viewpoint, the guidebook will refer to "compass-north," "compass-west," and so forth.

GPS Coordinates

GPS coordinates are provided for parking lots and key road crossings along the *AT*. The coordinates use North American Datum 83 (NAD83).

Undocumented Features

The separate waterproof hiking maps meant to accompany this guide generally reflect all the landmarks discussed here. Because the maps are extremely detailed, some features that appear on them, such as streams and old woods roads, may not be mentioned in the guidebook if they are not important landmarks. Other side trails that the hiker encounters may not be mentioned or mapped at all; in general, this is because the unmarked trails lead onto private property, and Trail managers wish to discourage their use.

TRAIL MAPS

Detailed maps of the *AT* are available for the entire area covered by this Guide. Their use is highly recommended.

The maps have been prepared by the Maps Committee of the PATC and are based on USGS maps. These 5-color, topographic maps indicate the route of the *AT* highlighted in contrasting color, side trails, shelters, cabins, highways, forest areas, and other major geographical features. Four PATC maps cover the *AT* in Maryland and northern Virginia. Maps 5 and 6 (both at 1:62,500 scale) are printed on the same sheet and are priced as one map. Map 7 is at 1:50,000 scale. Map 8 is at 1:62,500 scale. The area covered by each is as follows:

Map No.	State	Area
5	Maryland	Pen Mar to Turners Gap
6	Maryland	Turners Gap to Harpers Ferry
7	Va/W.Va	Harpers Ferry to Snickers Gap
8	Virginia	Snickers Gap to Chester Gap

The relevant PATC map is indicated under "Maps" for each section of the *AT*. PATC maps are available, for a reasonable charge, from the PATC headquarters in Vienna, Virginia, and various other distributors. These maps, like the Guide, are periodically revised. This edition of the Guide used the following map editions: PATC Map 5/6, Edition 19 (2013); PATC Map 7, Edition 16 (2013); and Map 8, Edition 15 (2013).

THE TRAIL

Trail Markings
The *AT* is marked by white paint blazes and various signs. In Harpers Ferry, however, the Park Service has banned markings along the town streets in the historic district. Look for markings on lampposts.

The paint blazes (2" by 6") have been placed at frequent intervals along the Trail. A double blaze (two blazes, one above the other) is placed as a warning sign. It may indicate a turn or change in direction that might otherwise not be noticed.

Maintained side trails are marked by similar blue blazes.

Important intersections are sometimes marked with wooden signs.

Trail Maintenance
The PATC is responsible for maintaining about 240 miles of *AT*, as well as blue-blazed side trails, from Pine Grove Furnace State Park in Pennsylvania through Shenandoah National Park. Within Maryland, Sections 1 and 2 are the responsibility of the Mountain Club of Maryland (Baltimore). In any case, all maintenance work is done by unpaid volunteers, usually with sub-sections assigned to individual overseers.

Trail Use

Those using the *AT* or side trails should not damage natural or man-made property, litter, or use trail bikes. Particular care should be taken to avoid fires. Smoking is discouraged, and fires should be built only at designated campsites. Camping should be done only at such campsites. Horseback riding requires specific permission of property owners and is forbidden in many areas.

Trail Relocations

Always follow the marked Trail. If it differs from the guidebook's Trail description, it is because the Trail was recently relocated in the area, probably to avoid a hazard or undesirable feature or to remove it from private property. If you use the old Trail, you may be trespassing and generating ill will toward the Trail community.

Information on Trail relocations between guidebook revisions is reported in ATC's magazine, Appalachian Trailway News, issued five times annually. Every effort has been made in this Guide to alert you to relocations that may occur. Do not follow new trails that are not blazed, because they may not yet be open to the public.

Water

Carrying water is necessary, and a one-quart container may not be enough, especially in dry seasons. The exertion of hiking, combined with water shortages, could lead to dehydration and increase fatigue, thus marring an otherwise enjoyable experience.

Although the *AT* may have sources of clean, potable water, any water source can become polluted. Most water sources along the Trail are unprotected and consequently very susceptible to contamination. All water should be purified by boiling, chemical treatment, or portable water filters before using. Take particular care to protect the purity of all water sources. Never wash dishes, clothes, or hands in the water source. Make sure food and human wastes are buried well away from any water source.

Weather

Heavy rainstorms are common in Maryland and northern Virginia. Tents should be thoroughly waterproof. A full-length poncho or rain suit and pack cover are essential; a short rain jacket is insufficient. In midsummer, avoid overexertion and protect your face, shoulders, and legs from sun.

Do not assume that winter weather in Maryland and northern Virginia will be mild. It can suddenly become extremely cold, with temperatures as low as zero degrees Fahrenheit for extended periods, especially at higher elevations. Considerable snowfalls can occur. Although the Trail in Maryland and northern Virginia usually can be traversed throughout the year, winter weather (December through March) can make travel and camping particularly difficult.

Equipment

The basic equipment rule is, never carry more than you need. Some items should be with you on every hike: the guidebook and maps; canteen; flashlight, even on day trips; whistle; emergency food; tissues; matches and fire starter; multipurpose knife; compass; rain gear; proper shoes and socks; warm, dry, spare clothes; and a first-aid kit. (See "First Aid Along the Trail.")

Take the time to consult periodicals, books, employees of outfitter stores, and other hikers before choosing the equipment that is best for you.

Getting Lost

Stop, if you have walked more than a quarter-mile (or roughly five minutes of hiking) without noticing a blaze or other Trail indicator. If you find no indication of the Trail, retrace your course until one appears. The cardinal mistake behind unfortunate experiences is insisting on continuing when the route seems obscure or dubious. Haste, even in a desire to reach camp before dark, only complicates the difficulty. When in doubt, remain where you are to avoid straying farther from the route.

Hiking long distances alone should be avoided. If undertaken, it requires extra precautions. A lone hiker who suffers a serious accident or illness might be risking death if he has not planned for the remote chance of isolation. Your destinations and estimated times of arrival should be known to someone who will initiate inquiries or a search if you do not appear when expected. On long trips, reporting your plans and progress every few days is a wise precaution.

A lone hiker who loses his way and chooses to bushwhack toward town runs considerable risks if an accident occurs. If he falls helpless away from a used trail, he might not be discovered for days or even weeks. Lone hikers are advised to stay on the Trail (or at least on a trail), even if it means spending an unplanned night in the woods in sight of a distant electric light. Your pack should always contain enough food and water to sustain you until daylight, when a careful retracing of your steps might lead you back to a safe route.

Distress Signals

An emergency call for distress consists of three short calls, audible or visible, repeated at regular intervals. A whistle is particularly good for audible signals. Visible signals may include, in daytime, light flashed with a mirror or smoke puffs; at night, a flashlight or three small bright fires.

Anyone recognizing such a signal should acknowledge it with two calls if possible, by the same method then go to the distressed person and determine the nature of the emergency. Arrange for more aid, if necessary.

Most of the *AT* is used enough that, if you are injured, you can expect to be found. However, if an area is remote and the weather bad, fewer hikers will be on the Trail. In this case, it might be best to study the Guide for the nearest place people are likely to be and attempt to move in that direction. If it is necessary to leave a heavy pack behind, be sure to take essentials, in case rescue is delayed. In bad weather, a night in the open without proper covering could be dangerous.

Rabies

Though rarely encountered, some individual mammals in Maryland and northern Virginia harbor rabies and therefore pose a serious danger to hikers.

Although raccoons have been the primary carriers, foxes, dogs, bats, and other mammals are potential carriers. All wild mammals should be avoided. Animals may carry the disease even though they show no symptoms. Unusual behavior by mammals should be reported to the authorities.

Transmission of rabies can occur from virtually any contact, even indirectly, from an inanimate object. Therefore, a danger is posed by raccoons tampering with packs and equipment. The usual precautions for hanging all equipment, by a rope, from a tree, should be followed.

Medical help should be sought immediately by anyone who believes he, or she, has had contact, direct or indirect, with a rabid animal.

Pests

Rattlesnakes and copperheads are found in Maryland and northern Virginia. See *"First Aid Along the Trail"* for the recommended treatment of snakebites.

Ticks, chiggers, no-see-ums, mosquitoes, and other insects could also be encountered. Carry repellent.

Poison ivy, stinging nettle, and briars grow along many sections of the Trail. Long pants are recommended. Trailside plants grow rapidly in spring and summer, and, although volunteers try to keep the Trail cleared, some places may be filled with dense growth by midsummer, especially where gypsy moths have destroyed the overstory vegetation.

Parking

Park in designated areas. If you leave your car parked overnight unattended, you may be risking theft or vandalism. Please do not ask Trail neighbors for permission to park your car near their homes.

Hunting

Hunting is prohibited in many state parks and on National Park Service lands whether acquired specifically for protection of the Appalachian Trail or as part of another unit of the national park system. Hunters who approach the *AT* from the side, and who do not know that they are on Trail lands, may also have no idea that the Trail is nearby. The

Trail traverses several other types of landownership, including national forest lands and state gamelands, on which hunting is allowed as part of the multiple-use management plan (national forests) or specifically for game (state gamelands).

Some hunting areas are marked by permanent or temporary signs, but any sign is subject to vandalism and removal. The prudent hiker, especially in the fall, makes himself aware of local hunting seasons and wears blaze orange during that time.

Trail Ethics

Please follow a few basic guidelines:

Do not cut, deface, or destroy trees, flowers, or any other natural or constructed feature.

Do not damage fences or leave gates open.

Do not litter. Carry out all trash. Do not bury it for animals or others to uncover.

Be careful with fire. Extinguish all burning material; a forest fire can start more easily than many realize.

In short: Take nothing but pictures, leave nothing but footprints, kill nothing but time.

Dogs are often a nuisance to other hikers. The territorial instincts of dogs often result in fights with other dogs. Dogs also frighten some hikers and chase wildlife. If a pet cannot be controlled, it should be left at home; otherwise, it will generate ill-will toward the Appalachian Trail and its users. Also, many at-home pets' muscles, foot pads, and sleeping habits are not adaptable to the rigors of *AT* hiking.

Keep to the defined Trail. Cutting across switchbacks, particularly on graded trails, disfigures the Trail, complicates route-finding, and causes erosion. The savings in time or distance are minimal; the damage is great. In areas where log walkways, steps, or rock treadway indicate special trail construction, take pains to use them. These have been installed to reduce trail-widening and erosion.

Group Hikes and Special Events

Special events, group hikes, or other group activities that could degrade the Appalachian Trail's natural or cultural resources or social values should be avoided. Examples of such activities include publicized spectator events, commercial or competitive activities, or programs involving large groups.

The policy of the Appalachian Trail Conservancy is that groups planning to spend one or more nights on the Trail should not exceed 10 people, and day-use groups should not exceed 25 people, unless the local maintaining organization has made special arrangements to both accommodate the group and protect Trail values.

FIRST AID ALONG THE TRAIL

by Robert Ohler, M.D., and the Appalachian Trail Conservancy

Hikers encounter a wide variety of terrain and climatic conditions along the Appalachian Trail. Prepare for the possibility of injuries. Some of the more common Trail-related medical problems are briefly discussed below.

Preparation is key to a safe trip. If possible, every hiker should take the free courses in advanced first aid and cardiopulmonary-resuscitation (CPR) techniques offered in most communities by the American Red Cross.

Even without this training, you can be prepared for accidents. Emergency situations can develop. Analyses of serious accidents have shown that a substantial number originate at home, in the planning stage of the trip.

Think about communications. Have you informed your relatives and friends about your expedition: locations, schedule, and time of return? Has all of your equipment been carefully checked? Considering the season and altitude, have you provided for water, food, and shelter?

While hiking, set your own comfortable pace. If you are injured or lost or a storm strikes, stop. Remember, your brain is your most important survival tool. Inattention can start a chain of events leading to disaster.

If an accident occurs, treat the injury first. If outside help is needed, at least one person should stay with the injured hiker. Two people should go for help and carry with them notes on the exact location of the accident, what has been done to aid the injured, and what help is needed.

The injured will need encouragement, assurances of help, and confidence in your competence. Treat him gently. Keep him supine, warm, and quiet. Protect him from the weather with insulation below and above him. Examine him carefully, noting all possible injuries.

General Emergencies

Back or neck injuries: Immobilize the victim's entire body, where he lies. Protect head and neck from movement if the neck is injured, and treat as a fracture. Transportation must be on a rigid frame, such as a litter or a door. The spinal cord could be severed by inexpert handling. This type of injury must be handled by a large group of experienced personnel. Obtain outside help.

Bleeding: Stop the flow of blood by using a method appropriate to the amount and type of bleeding. Exerting pressure over the wound with the fingers, with or without a dressing, may be sufficient. Minor arterial bleeding can be controlled with local pressure and bandaging. Major arterial bleeding might require compressing an artery against a bone to stop the flow of blood. Elevate the arm or legs above the heart. To stop bleeding from an artery in the leg, place a hand in the groin and press toward the inside of the leg. Stop arterial bleeding from an arm by placing a hand between the armpit and elbow and pressing toward the inside of the arm.

Apply a tourniquet only if you are unable to control severe bleeding by pressure and elevation. Warning: This method should be used only when the limb will be lost anyway. Once applied, a tourniquet should only be removed by medical personnel equipped to stop the bleeding by other means and to restore lost blood. The tourniquet should be located between the wound and the heart. If there is a traumatic amputation (loss of hand, leg, or foot), place the tourniquet two inches above the amputation.

Blisters: Good boot fit, without points of irritation or pressure, should be proven before a hike. Always keep feet dry while hiking. Prevent blisters by responding early to any discomfort. Place adhesive tape or moleskin over areas of developing redness or soreness. If irritation can be relieved, allow blister fluid to be reabsorbed. If a blister forms and continued irritation makes draining it necessary, wash the area with soap and water and prick the edge of the blister with a needle that has been sterilized by the flame of a match. Bandage with a sterile gauze pad and moleskin.

Dislocation of a leg or arm joint: This is extremely painful. Do not try to put it back in place. Immobilize the entire limb with splints in the position it is found.

Exhaustion: This is caused by inadequate food consumption, dehydration and salt deficiency, overexertion, or all three. The victim may lose motivation, slow down, gasp for air, complain of weakness, dizziness, nausea, or headache. Treat by feeding, especially carbohydrates. Slowly replace lost water (normal fluid intake should be two to four quarts per day). Give salt dissolved in water (one teaspoon per cup). In the case of overexertion, rest is essential.

Fractures of legs, ankles, or arms: Splint before moving the victim. After treating wounds, use any available material that will offer firm support, such as tree branches or boards. Pad each side of the arm or leg with soft material, supporting and immobilizing the joints above and below the injury. Bind the splints together with strips of cloth. Transport the victim to a medical facility for treatment.

Shock: Expect shock after all injuries. It is a potentially fatal depression of bodily functions that is made more critical with improper handling, cold, fatigue, and anxiety. Relieve the pain as quickly as possible. Do not administer aspirin if severe bleeding is present; Tylenol or other non-aspirin pain relievers are safe to give.

Look for nausea, paleness, trembling, sweating, or thirst. Lay the hiker flat on his back, and raise his feet slightly, or position him, if he can be safely moved, so his head is down the slope. Protect him from the wind, and keep him as warm as possible. A campfire will help.

Sprains: Look or feel for soreness or swelling. Bandage and treat as a fracture. Cool and raise joint.

Wounds (except eye wounds): Clean wound with soap and water. If possible, apply a clean dressing to protect the wound from further contamination.

Chilling and Freezing Emergencies

Every hiker should be familiar with the symptoms, treatment, and methods of preventing the common and sometimes fatal condition of *hypothermia*. Wind chill and/or body wetness, particularly aggravated by fatigue and hunger, can rapidly drain body heat to dangerously low levels. This often occurs at temperatures well above freezing. Shivering, lethargy, mental slowing, and confusion are early symptoms of hypothermia, which can begin without the victim realizing it and, if untreated, can lead to death.

Always keep dry, spare clothing and a water-repellent windbreaker in your pack, and wear a hat in chilling weather. Wet clothing loses much of its insulating value, although wet wool is warmer than other wet fabrics. Always, when in chilling conditions, suspect the onset of hypothermia.

To treat this potentially fatal condition, immediately seek shelter and warm the entire body, preferably by placing it in a sleeping bag and administering warm liquids. The addition of another person's body heat may aid in warming.

A sign of *frostbite* is grayish or waxy, yellow-white spots on the skin. The frozen area will be numb. To thaw, warm the frozen part by direct contact with bare flesh. When first frozen, a cheek, nose, or chin can often be thawed by covering with a hand taken from a warm glove. Superficially frostbitten hands sometimes can be thawed by placing them under armpits, on the stomach, or between the thighs. With a partner, feet can be treated similarly. Do not rub frozen flesh.

Frozen layers of deeper tissue beneath the skin are characterized by a solid, "woody" feeling and an inability to move the flesh over bony prominences. Tissue loss is minimized by rapid rewarming of the area in water slightly below 105 degrees Fahrenheit (measure accurately with a thermometer).

Thawing of a frozen foot should not be attempted until the patient has been evacuated to a place where rapid, controlled thawing can take place. Walking on a frozen foot is entirely possible and does not cause increased damage. Walking after thawing is impossible.

Never rewarm over a stove or fire. This "cooks" flesh and results in extensive loss of tissue.

Treatment of a deep freezing injury after rewarming must be done in a hospital.

Heat Emergencies

Exposure to extremely high temperatures, high humidity, and direct sunlight can cause health problems.

Heat cramps are usually caused by strenuous activity in high heat and humidity, when sweating depletes salt levels in blood and tissues. Symptoms are intermittent cramps in legs and abdominal wall and painful spasms of muscles. Pupils of eyes may dilate with each spasm. The skin becomes cold and clammy. Treat with rest and salt dissolved in water (one teaspoon of salt per glass).

Heat exhaustion, caused by physical exercise during prolonged exposure to heat, is a breakdown of the body's heat-regulating system. The circulatory system is disrupted, reducing the supply of blood to vital organs such as the brain, heart, and lungs. The victim can have heat cramps and sweat heavily. Skin is moist and cold with face flushed, then pale. Pulse can be unsteady and blood pressure low. He may vomit and be delirious. Place the victim in shade, flat on his back, with feet 8-12 inches higher than head. Give him sips of salt water—half a glass every 15 minutes for about an hour. Loosen his clothes. Apply cold cloths.

Heat stroke and **sun stroke** are caused by the failure of the heat-regulating system to cool the body by sweating. They are emergency, life-threatening conditions. Body temperature can rise to 106 degrees or higher. Symptoms include weakness, nausea, headache, heat cramps, exhaustion, body temperature rising rapidly, pounding pulse, and high blood pressure. The victim may be delirious or comatose. Sweating will stop before heat stroke becomes apparent. Armpits may be dry and skin flushed and pink, then turning ashen or purple in later stages. Move victim to cool place immediately. Cool the body in any way possible (e.g., sponging). Body temperature must be regulated artificially from outside of the body until the heat-regulating system can be rebalanced. Be careful not to overchill once temperature goes below 102 degrees.

Heat weakness is characterized by fatigue, headache, mental and physical inefficiency, heavy sweating, high pulse rate, and general weakness. Drink plenty of water, find as cool a spot as possible, keep quiet, and replenish salt loss.

Sunburn causes redness of the skin, discoloration, swelling, and pain. It occurs rapidly and can be severe at higher elevations. It can be prevented by applying a commercial sun screen; zinc oxide is the most effective. Treat by protecting from further exposure and covering the area with ointment and a dressing. Give the victim large amounts of fluids.

Artificial Respiration

Artificial respiration might be required when an obstruction constricts the air passages or after respiratory failure caused by air being depleted of oxygen, such as after electrocution, by drowning, or because of toxic gases in the air. Quick action is necessary if the victim's lips, fingernail beds, or tongue have become blue; if he is unconscious; or if the pupils of his eyes become enlarged.

If food or a foreign body is lodged in the air passage and coughing is ineffective, try to remove it with the fingers. If the foreign body is inaccessible, grasp the victim from behind, and with one hand hold the opposite wrist just below the breastbone. Squeeze rapidly and firmly, expelling air forcibly from the lungs to expel the foreign body. Repeat this maneuver two to three times, if necessary.

If breathing stops, administer artificial respiration, as air can be forced around the obstruction into the lungs. The mouth-to-mouth, or mouth-to-nose, method of forcing air into the victim's lungs should be used. The preferred method is:

1. Clear the victim's mouth of any obstructions.
2. Place one hand under the victim's neck and lift.
3. Place heel of other hand on the forehead, and tilt head backwards.

(Maintain this position during procedure.) Use thumb and index finger to pinch nostrils.

4. Open your mouth, and make a seal with it over victim's mouth. If the victim is a small child, cover both the nose and the mouth.

5. Breathe deeply, and blow out about every five seconds, or 12 breaths a minute.

6. Watch victim's chest for expansion.

7. Listen for exhalation.

Poison Ivy

Poison ivy is the most common plant found along the Trail that irritates the skin. It is most often found as a vine trailing near the ground or climbing on fences or trees, sometimes up to 20 feet from the ground. A less common variety that is often unrecognized is an erect shrub, standing alone and unsupported, up to 10 feet tall.

The leaves are in clusters of three, the end leaf with a longer stalk and pointed tip, light green in spring but darkening as the weeks pass. The inconspicuous flowers are greenish; the berries white or cream. The irritating oil is in all parts of the plant, even in dead plants, and is carried in the smoke of burning plants. Those who believe themselves immune may find that they are seriously susceptible if the concentration is great enough or the toxins are ingested.

If you have touched poison ivy, wash immediately with strong soap (but not with one containing added oil). If a rash develops in the next day or so, treat it with calamine lotion or Solarcaine. Do not scratch. If blisters become serious or the rash spreads to the eyes, see a doctor.

Lyme Disease

Lyme disease is carried by *Borrelia burgdorferi,* a spirochete form of bacteria, and is transmitted by the bite of a deer tick, an insect about 3 mm in size. These ticks feed during one stage of their life cycle on deer, but they can also be found on birds, field mice, and other rodents.

Hikers should be aware of the symptoms and monitor themselves and their partners for signs of the disease. Inspect for tick bites at the end of each day, wear light-colored clothing so you can spot and brush off ticks; if you are bitten by a tick, remove the tick immediately by grasping it as close to the skin as possible with tweezers and tugging gently. When treated early, Lyme disease usually can be cured with antibiotics.

The early signs of Lyme disease are a rash at the site of the tick bite with a red circle and a clear center, flu-like symptoms, such as sore throat, severe fatigue, chills, headaches, fever, muscle aches, stiff neck, appetite loss, nausea, vomiting, diarrhea, and abdominal cramps. However, one-quarter of all people with an infected tick bite show none of the early symptoms.

If the disease is not treated in its early stage, serious complications involving the heart, joints and nervous system, may appear months or years later. These symptoms may be arthritic complications such as hot, swollen and painful joints, muscles, tendons and shooting pains in the arms and legs. Heart complications such as irregular heartbeat, chest pain, fainting, dizziness, and shortness of breath, also become evident. Neurological complications may arise, such as facial paralysis, abnormal skin sensations and sensitivities, insomnia, and hearing loss. The psychological complications, including mood changes, memory and concentration problems, depression and dementia, are often mistaken for mental illness. Lyme disease can also be misdiagnosed as rheumatoid arthritis, meningitis, or multiple sclerosis. The disease is rarely fatal, but heart complications may cause life-threatening arrhythmias, and infection during pregnancy may cause miscarriage.

If you suspect you have been bitten by an infected tick, consult your doctor who will be able to determine if you've been infected, and provide proper treatment if necessary.

Lightning Strikes

Although the odds of being struck by lightning are low, 200 to 400 people a year are killed by lightning in the United States. Respect the force of lightning, and seek shelter during a storm.

Do not start a hike if thunderstorms are likely. If caught in a storm, immediately find shelter. Hard-roofed automobiles or large buildings are best; tents and convertible automobiles offer no protection. When indoors, stay away from windows, open doors, fireplaces, and large metal objects. Do not hold a potential lightning rod, such as a fishing pole. Avoid tall structures, such as ski lifts, flagpoles, powerline towers, and the tallest trees or hilltops. If you cannot enter a building or car, take shelter in a stand of smaller trees. Avoid clearings. If caught in the open, crouch down, or roll into a ball. If you are in water, get out. Spread out groups, so that everyone is not struck by a single bolt.

If a person is struck by lightning or splashed by a charge hitting a nearby object, the victim will probably be thrown, perhaps a great distance. Clothes can be burned or torn. Metal objects (such as belt buckles) may become hot, and shoes can be blown off. The victim often has severe muscle contractions (which can cause breathing difficulties), confusion, and temporary blindness or deafness. In more severe cases, the victim may have feathered or sunburst patterns of burns over the skin or ruptured eardrums. He may lose consciousness or breathe irregularly. Occasionally, victims stop breathing and suffer cardiac arrest.

If someone is struck by lightning, perform artificial respiration and CPR until emergency technicians arrive or you can transport the injured to a hospital. Lightning victims may be unable to breathe independently for 15 to 30 minutes but can recover quickly once they can breathe on their own. Do not give up early; a seemingly lifeless individual can be saved if you breathe for him promptly after the strike.

Assume that the victim was thrown a great distance; protect the spine, treat other injuries, then transport him to the hospital.

Hantavirus

Federal and state health authorities have tested various sites in Virginia looking for infected deer mice, the principal carriers of Hantavirus in the East, but found no mice infected with the virus, which apparently is most often picked up when it is airborne. (The virus travels from an infected rodent through its evaporating urine, droppings and saliva into the air.)

Hantavirus is extremely rare and difficult to "catch." Prevention measures for thru-hikers are relatively simple: Air out a closed, mice-infested structure for an hour before occupying it; don't sleep on mouse droppings (use a mat or tent); don't handle mice; treat your water; wash your hands if you think you have handled droppings.

If you are truly concerned about hantavirus, call ATC for a fact sheet.

Snakebites

Hikers on the Appalachian Trail may encounter copperheads or timber rattlesnakes on their journey. These are pit vipers, characterized by triangular heads, vertical elliptical pupils, two or less hinged fangs on the front part of the jaw (fangs are replaced every six to 10 weeks), heat-sensory facial pits on the sides of the head, and a single row of scales on the underbelly by the tail.

The best way to avoid being bitten by poisonous snakes is to avoid their known habitats and avoid reaching into dark areas (use a walking stick to move suspicious objects). Do not hike alone or at night in snake territory; always have a flashlight and walking stick. Do not handle snakes. A dead snake can bite and envenomate you with a reflex action for 20 to 60 minutes after death.

Not all snakebites result in envenomation, even if the snake is poisonous. The signs of envenomation are one or more fang marks in addition to rows of teeth marks, burning pain, and swelling at the bite (swelling usually begins within five to 10 minutes of envenomation and can become very severe). Lips, face, and scalp may tingle and become numb 30 to 60 minutes after the bite. (If these symptoms are immediate and the victim is frightened and excited, then they are most likely due to hyperventilation). Thirty to 90 minutes after the bite, the victim's eyes and mouth may twitch, and he may have a rubbery or metallic taste in his mouth. He may sweat, experience weakness, nausea and vomiting, or faint one to two hours after the bite. Bruising at the bite usually begins within two to three hours, and large blood blisters may develop within six to 10 hours. The victim may have difficulty breathing, have bloody urine, vomit blood, and may collapse six to 12 hours after the bite.

If someone you are with has been bitten by a snake, act quickly. The definitive treatment for snake-venom poisoning is the proper administration of antivenom. Get the victim to a hospital immediately. Keep the victim calm. Increased activity can spread the venom and the illness. Retreat out of snake's striking range, but try to identify it so the authorities can estimate the amount of antivenom necessary.

Immediately transport the victim to the nearest hospital. If possible, splint the body part that was bitten, to avoid unnecessary motion. If a limb was bitten, keep it at a level below the heart. Do not apply ice directly to the wound. If it will take longer than two hours to reach medical help, and the bite is on an arm or leg, place a 2"x 2", 1/4"- thick cloth pad over the bite and firmly wrap the limb (ideally with an elastic wrap) directly over the bite and six inches on either side, taking care to check for adequate circulation to the fingers and toes. This wrap may slow the spread of venom.

First-Aid Kit

The following kit is suggested for those who have had no first-aid or other medical training. It weighs about a pound, and occupies about a 3"x 6" x 9" space.

Eight 4" x 4" gauze pads	One triangular bandage (40")
Five 2" bandages	Two 3" rolls of gauze
Four 3" x 4" gauze pads	Ten large butterfly closures
Ten 1" bandages	One 15' roll of 2" adhesive tape
Six alcohol prep pads	One 3" Ace bandage
One tweezers	Twenty salt tablets
One small scissors	Three safety pins
One 3" x 4" moleskin	Personal medications as necessary
Twenty tablets of aspirin-free pain killer	

SELECTED REFERENCES

Red Cross first-aid manuals.

Mountaineering First Aid: A Guide to Accident Response and First Aid (Seattle: The Mountaineers, 1985).

Emergency Survival Handbook, by the American Safety League (1985). A pocket-sized book and survival kit with easy instructions.

Medicine for the Outdoors: A Guide to Emergency Medical Procedures and First Aid, by Paul S. Auerbach, M.D. (Boston: Little Brown, 1986.)

South Mountain Outcrop   Larry Broadwell

GEOLOGY ALONG THE TRAIL

by Collins Chew

The Appalachian Mountains have a long and fascinating history. Much that is known about geology and mountains was discovered through the study of the long, often straight, ridges in this area. If the Appalachian Mountains are thought of as a book, several interesting chapters may be read by observant people hiking along the Appalachian Trail in Maryland and northern Virginia.

Another mountain range stood "here" before the Appalachians. "Here" meaning that the rocks of those ancient mountains now lie under much of Eastern North America. The continent then, 1.1 billion years ago, was south of the equator. (The surface of the earth is made up of a number of thin, relatively rigid "plates," which move about the earth's surface at the speed our fingernails grow, an inch or two each year.) At that time, the North American Plate collided with (probably) the western side of the South American Plate, and the mountains formed as the two plates slowly crushed into each other. Those old rocks have been heated and changed several times; they are coarsely crystalline (crystals visible to the naked eye) with white minerals (mostly quartz and feldspar) and dark minerals (often mica and hornblende). Often the minerals are found in light and dark bands that show how a hot, somewhat softened, rock flowed slowly like putty at great depth and under intense pressure. Great movements since that time have left large, generally narrow slivers of that rock in place within the Appalachian Mountains. It so happens that one short section of the Appalachian Trail crosses a narrow band of this 1.1 billion-year-old rock around Sandy Hook Bridge, between Weverton Cliffs and Maryland Heights. The Trail here follows the towpath of the old Chesapeake & Ohio Canal, and little if any of the old rock can be seen, but the adjacent Pleasant Valley lies on these rocks that once lay under ancient mountains.

No records were left here for several hundred million years as those mountains eroded away. About 800 million years ago, the great land mass began to pull apart into separate continents again. During the next 200 million years, faults broke up the land, and mountain-size areas tilted, sank, or rose. Great outpourings of dark, very fluid, basalt lava formed extensive sheets of black rock. A few explosive volcanoes erupted lighter lava and ash. Records of this time, centered about 700 million years ago, are found in those old lava flows, although chemical changes have altered the black basalt to greenstone, a dark gray-green rock. In many places, this dark rock breaks along straight lines at sharp angles, which gives the rock a very craggy appearance. The rock weathers to clayey soil containing rock chips. These old lava flows are found from the northern edge of Tennessee to Pennsylvania. They lie under the Appalachian Trail of Maryland and northern Virginia in short sections at the trail to Buzzard Knob, at Foxville Road, from Washington Monument State Park to Turners Gap, and in spots between Wilson Gap and Ashby Gap. The southern 23 miles of this section, from Ashby Gap to Shenandoah National Park, is on this dark rock. Darker spots and holes in the rock show where minerals filled former gas bubbles in the molten rock. White quartz and light green epidote are found in the spots and in veins that make striking lines in the dark rock. Between Wolfsville Road and Raven Rock Road is a short section underlain by red volcanic rock typical of the explosive volcanoes.

An ocean somewhat like the Atlantic Ocean formed to what is now the east. It is called the Iapetus Ocean. Erosion wore away the mountains of North America, and the rocks cooled, became denser, and sank lower in the crust. The shallow sea at the edge of the ocean gradually covered the continent, and a sand beach formed along the shore. Eventually additional deposits covered the sand and turned it into hard quartzite, which still shows the sand grains and pebbles from which it formed. In many places, lines in the rock show where little sand bars grew. Each tide or rain washed a little more sand over the edge to make a new layer. These beds, which lie at an angle to the general bedding plane of the rock, are called crossbeds. The quartzite is extremely hard and resistant to erosion. White quartz veins create striking elongated patterns in the quartzite. These veins formed as deposits from solutions that flowed through cracks after the main body or rock had been laid down.

Generally found under ridges, the quartzite underlies all of the Appalachian Trail in this area except at the locations mentioned above and in Harpers Ferry, West Virginia. Many cliffs are composed of this quartzite, which appears more blocky than the greenstone. It weathers to sand. In places the ridge is flat, and it is puzzling why it is not farmland. The answer lies in the relatively sterile sand, which holds few nutrients and little water. In some locations, streaks of sand alternate with black humus. The sand and humus do not seem to mix well. Even in the absence of surface rock, the change of bedrock from quartzite to greenstone can be noticed where the surface sand gives way to dirt and clay containing rock chips. Some small beds of shale (formed from hardened mud) do lie within the quartzite, but they are infrequently obvious along the *AT*. These rocks formed about 550 million years ago.

As the sea grew deeper, clear water covered the sand, and limestone formed over it. Occasionally mud washed in from the center of the continent. Although limestone and mud covered large areas of the Eastern United States, it is evident in only one place in our section of the *AT*. Beds laid down as mud were changed to slate, which shows in Harpers Ferry and as ledges in the rivers there. Earth movements imparted a wavy pattern to some of the slate near the town. This is the youngest rock under the *AT* in this area and is over 500 million years old.

The Iapetus Ocean narrowed as part of the crust sank at an angle under other crust, and islands were brought against North America. These islands of a land called Avalon became much of the Piedmont Plateau to the east of the *AT*. Erosion of these new eastern lands covered our area with deep layers of sand and mud. Later, perhaps 250 million years ago, North Africa slowly collided with North America, crushing a large area of these sediments, causing once flat beds to become rippled in huge folds and sliding some areas over others as great faults broke the rock. To the south, tens of miles of rock layers slid over others in a manner likened to roof shingles being pushed over one another. The beds of rocks under the Appalachian Trail here were turned to steep angles or were even overturned. Relative to each other, the rocks have had little movement since that time. The beds now tend to line up nearly in a north-northeast to south-southwest direction.

Since then, erosion averaging perhaps an inch per thousand years has removed thousands of feet of rock to expose the surface we see today. The more resistant beds (most frequently quartzite) erode at slower rates and are left as ridges, whereas the limestones and shales erode to the valleys that parallel the *AT*. Greenstone varies somewhat from place to place and can be fairly resistant. It forms some of the mountains. The long ridges generally trace the upturned edges of quartzite. One side of the ridge may parallel the upper surface of the quartzite and have at the top a cliff that faces the other side of the mountain. The hardest quartzite is relatively thin, and softer rock underlies it. When this softer rock erodes from under the quartzite, the top edge breaks off and rolls down the mountain, leaving the cliff. In places in Maryland, the *AT* follows the level surface of a shelf beside the cliff. This is an unusual feature, common only in Maryland and nearby Pennsylvania. The relatively even tops of the ridges were once thought to be the remains of a level plain, called a peneplain, but it is now thought that the quartzite erodes too fast to be the remnant of a plain that existed millions of years ago. Nevertheless, gradual uplift has sustained the mountains' elevation, although periods of slower uplift may have let erosion predominate and allowed the mountains to be nearly eroded away for a time. These periods of unchecked erosion may have contributed to the comparatively even ridgetops; however, the changing rates of uplift and erosion are not very well understood. It is thought that uplift and erosion are nearly balanced now, so that the mountains maintain a nearly constant elevation.

Almost 200 million years ago, Africa (and, to the north, Europe) began to pull away from North America. By 160 million years ago, a narrow Atlantic Ocean had appeared. (It continues to grow wider as measured by satellites.) New ocean floor formed as black basalt lava oozed out of cracks along the Mid-Atlantic Ridge. The nearby ocean became the low point and provided short steep paths along which new rivers washed away sediment from the mountains. The Potomac River drained a particularly large area, and its power allowed it to cut the deep canyon we see at Harpers Ferry. The Shenandoah River was originally a small tributary of the Potomac. In flowing into the deep gorge of the Potomac, however, the Shenandoah cut down swiftly and enlarged its valley until it captured the headwaters of many other smaller streams that once crossed the Blue Ridge and flowed directly into the Atlantic Ocean. The low points of the ridge—such as Keys Gap, Ashby Gap, and Chester Gap—once held streams that flowed across the Blue Ridge. After the Shenandoah River captured their headwaters, the slow uplift overcame erosion and lifted the gaps above the surrounding valleys.

In the last few million years, great ice sheets have occasionally advanced from the north, but they never quite reached our area. (They did reach central Pennsylvania.) The freezing times helped break up the rocks and, in a few places, the frost heave action caused rocks to separate by size. This led to the formation of boulder fields such as the Devils Racecourses, which resemble, and are called, "rock rivers." These boulder fields once moved slowly and may yet be moved a bit by ice that forms under them. Lichens, and later trees, grow on these rocks as the movement stops.

The topography we see today resulted from a long period of erosion working on the very slowly rising land, a process that accentuated the differences in rocks with differing resistance. This process continues today.

POTOMAC APPALACHIAN TRAIL CLUB (PATC)

The Potomac Appalachian Trail Club (PATC), founded in November 1927, is one of the 31 organizations maintaining the Appalachian Trail under the Appalachian Trail Conservancy. It is also the third largest in number of members (more than 7,200) being surpassed only by the Appalachian Mountain Club in Boston and the Green Mountain Club in Vermont, both older organizations.

Altogether, the PATC is responsible for maintaining 240 miles of the Appalachian Trail and over 900 miles of other trails. Within SNP, this includes the entire length of the *AT*, and over 60% of the side trails. In 2014, the PATC contributed more than 43,000 hours of volunteer trail work to various government organizations. More than 600 volunteer trail, shelter and cabin overseers performed this work. During any given day of the year, it is likely that a PATC overseer is working somewhere inside the Park.

PATC maintains side trails in George Washington National Forest and has developed a 251-mile side trail known as the Tuscarora Trail running from the North District of SNP through Hancock, MD, and reconnecting with the *AT* north of Carlisle, PA. As noted earlier, PATC also maintains a network of shelters and cabins.

PATC publishes two guides for the *AT*—this guide, and the *Appalachian Trail Guide: Shenandoah National Park with Side Trails*. The guidebook for PATC's portion of the *AT* in Pennsylvania is covered in a guide published by the Keystone Trails Association (KTA), of which PATC is a member. PATC also publishes numerous other guides for areas within the northern Virginia /Maryland/West Virginia/ Pennsylvania area. The Club issues a number of historical publications prepared by members as well as the maps and guides previously cited. This includes several books on history in the Shenandoah National Park. The PATC also issues a monthly newsletter, the *Potomac Appalachian*. A complete list of publications, with prices, may be obtained from PATC

Headquarters, 118 Park St., SE, Vienna, VA 22180-4609, or on the web (www.patc.net). The PATC also maintains an up-to-date website, described below. The Club has an active Mountaineering Section, which offers assistance and training in rock climbing techniques, as well as more difficult climbing opportunities for the advanced climber. Information on their weekly activities can be found at www.potomacmountainclub.org.

The Ski Touring Section conducts workshops for beginners, participates in work trips to improve ski trails in local areas and organizes ski trips to local and distant ski areas. These, as well as other activities, are described in UPSLOPE, the Section's monthly newsletter. Visit their website at www.patc.us/chapters/ski.

The Shenandoah Mountain Rescue Group is a semi-professional group of volunteers dedicated to wilderness search and rescue and outdoor safety education. The group meets twice a month at PATC Headquarters and conducts frequent training workshops in the field. More information is at www.smrg.org.

A select group of members participates in PATC's Trail Patrol, which makes regular patrols within the Park and PATC's remaining trail region. The Trail Patrol is available in the backcountry to assist hikers and backpackers and provide information on trail routes and conditions.

If you live in the Washington, D.C., region, a call or letter to PATC can provide you with information on trail, shelter, and cabin work trips, as well as many other activities conducted by the Club. A monthly newsletter, *Potomac Appalachian*, is mailed to all members listing Club activities, including hikes and work trips. For general information call 703-242-0315. The PATC website, www.patc.net, also contains a calendar of events that include hikes and work trips.

PATC WEB SITE

PATC's web site was the second volunteer trail club web site posted on the Internet – following the Appalachian Mountain Club web site by one month.

From the time of its appearance in 1995, the site has expanded dramatically. The PATC web site now contains complete information about the Club and its activities, including secure online ordering for maps, publications, and guidebooks. The site also contains complete information about renting and using the Club's public and "member-only" cabins. Cabin reservations can be made online. There is also a significant amount of information that can enhance your outdoor experiences, including Indian history, early human history of explorations in the region, and early Club history that documents PATC's early trail-building activities.

PATC suggests you visit the web site's home page and locate the resources mentioned using the available hyperlinks. The URL to the PATC web site is: http://www.patc.net. The clubs Facebook page can be accessed from the PATC website.

Appalachian Trail marker   Laurie Potteiger

Overview of *AT* Location in Maryland

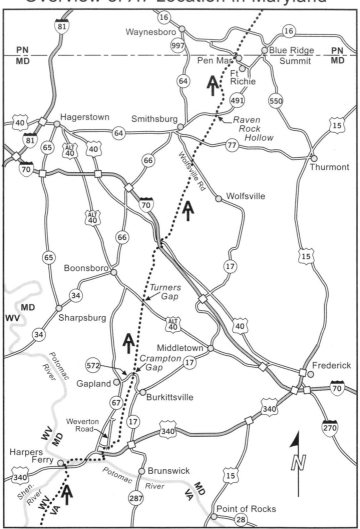

MARYLAND

GENERAL INFORMATION
Distance: 40.9 Miles

The *AT* follows the crest of South Mountain, a name applied to a succession of narrow ridges, from the Pennsylvania line to the Potomac River. Along the river, the Trail is located on the old Chesapeake & Ohio Canal towpath, now part of the Chesapeake & Ohio Canal National Historical Park. From the towpath, the Trail crosses the Potomac on the Goodloe Byron Memorial Footbridge. The continuation of South Mountain across the river, known as Short Hill Mountain, dwindles and becomes indistinguishable among the low foothills of northern Virginia. The Trail is therefore located on a parallel ridge to the west, Blue Ridge Mountain, which forms the boundary between Virginia and West Virginia. Similarly, the extension of Blue Ridge Mountain into Maryland is known as Elk Ridge, which continues north as far as Crampton Gap. Both Elk Ridge and South Mountain are part of the Blue Ridge Mountains of Maryland.

South Mountain is mostly covered with hardwoods, and the slopes drain into the tributaries of the Potomac. The numerous viewpoints along the Trail include Pen Mar, High Rock, Black Rock Cliffs, Annapolis Rocks, Monument Knob, White Rocks, Crampton Gap, and Weverton Cliffs. South of Monument Knob, the Trail is rich in Civil War history.

In Maryland, the elevation of the *AT* on South Mountain varies from 930 feet at Crampton Gap, to about 1,880 feet in multiple locations further north. Lambs Knoll, 1,772 feet, dominates the southern part of the ridge.

The Maryland portion of the Trail has been divided into the following sections:

1. Pen Mar to Raven Rock Hollow 5.9 mi
2. Raven Rock Hollow to Wolfsville Road 4.1 mi
3. Wolfsville Road to Interstate 70 8.6 mi
4. Interstate 70 to Turners Gap 4.9 mi
5. Turners Gap to Crampton Gap 7.4mi
6. Crampton Gap to Weverton 6.7 mi
7. Weverton to Harpers Ferry 3.3 mi

Since South Mountain is now a state park along its entire length in Maryland, camping is permitted only in designated areas and open fires only in fireplaces provided.

GROUP CAMPING: Any group of more than ten persons planning to camp in South Mountain State Park should call or write in advance to: Park Manager, South Mountain State Park, 21843 National Pike, Boonsboro, MD 21713. Phone: 301-791-4767.

HISTORY ALONG THE TRAIL

The rich history and colorful folklore of the Trail in Maryland compensate for its lack of spectacular scenic grandeur.

Early History

South Mountain served as a barrier that contributed to a pattern of north and south migration by the aborigines. Unlike the open country of the western plains and eastern ridges of the Rocky Mountains, where the edges of open ridges provided the safest travel for the Indians, the crest of South Mountain was not, according to tradition, used by the Indians. The Indians followed the Monocacy Trail from Pennsylvania, crossing the Potomac at Noland's Ferry. The Monocacy Trail is sometimes called the Warriors Path. On the west side of South Mountain, the Delaware Indians in the north and the Catawbas from the south followed the Antietam and Conococheague Creek valleys, crossing the Potomac at their deltas. Here their battles continued after the arrival of the first white men. In the 1730s and 1740s, these valleys became the corridors for German immigrants arriving in the port of Philadelphia bound for the Shenandoah Valley and other parts of Virginia where Lord Fairfax offered inducements for settlement.

A few trappers and settlers crossed South Mountain in the 1720s and 1730s. Israel Friend was mining ore on both sides of the Potomac near the mouth of Antietam Creek in the late 1720s, and a few settlers were farming along Antietam Creek in the 1730s. By 1732, the Lord Proprietor (Lord Baltimore) caused surveys to be made and began to grant lands on the west side of South Mountain. Comparative safety from the Indians awaited the Treaty of Lancaster in 1744, followed by the purchase of land from the Indians by the colony of Maryland. The Treaty of Lancaster with the Six Nations permitted the Indians to travel through Maryland from Pennsylvania to the Carolinas and established a temporary boundary between Maryland and Pennsylvania as far west as two miles above the source of the Potomac. For three hundred pounds sterling, the Indians provided a quit claim to lands east of this location.

Locations of Early Crossings of South Mountain

The earliest traverse of the South Mountain barrier in Maryland seems to have been along the Potomac, where neutral territory was maintained by the Indian tribes during the spring run of the yellow suckers. This gap through the Blue Ridge became the earliest thoroughfare of explorers and trappers. Louis Michelle and an exploring party from Annapolis crossed here in 1707. By 1733 Peter Stephens was operating ferries across both the Potomac and Shenandoah rivers at this gap in the Blue Ridge, and Peter Hoffman, a peddler from Baltimore, was making stops at the Stephens trading post on his route between Frederick and the German settlements in the upper Shenandoah Valley. A foldboat for use on western rivers was produced in the government shops at Harpers Ferry and collected by the Lewis and Clark Expedition (1804-1806) at the beginning of their trip. Later the canal and railroad followed the wagon road when the settlers pushed westward toward the Ohio. Both were in operation in this section by the end of 1834.

The first road to cross the ridge to reach the frontier was Israel Friend's Mill Road through Crampton Gap. The crossing through Turners Gap was a foot and horse path until General Braddock's army built a road in 1755 for his wagon train and personal carriage. Passenger stagecoach service across the gap was inaugurated on August 1, 1797. Several sessions of the Maryland legislature provided funds for the improvement of the road; in 1806 Turners Gap was designated the route of the National Road, and Federal improvements followed. By the 1850s, traffic on the National Road had declined, with the railroads and canal absorbing the freight and passenger traffic.

Old South Mountain Inn at Turners Gap, which still operates as a tavern (meals and drinks), is one of the oldest public houses along the *AT*. The date of the first tavern in Turners Gap cannot be determined, but the construction of the present building has been estimated as early as 1732 and as late as 1780. It had 22 rooms to rent, and at the height of the traffic on the National Road it employed blacksmiths to repair wagons and shoe horses around the clock and kept relay horses in the stables to relieve those exhausted from the steep grade. Abraham Lincoln spent a night at the tavern while on his way to take his seat in Congress, and it was reportedly a favorite hangout of Daniel Webster and Henry Clay. Presidents Jackson, William Henry Harrison, Polk, Taylor, and Van Buren passed through Turners Gap when traveling the National Road, and some of them may have stayed overnight in the tavern.

Mrs. Dahlgren, widow of Admiral John A. Dahlgren, commandant of the Washington Navy Yard during the Civil War and credited with perfecting the rifled cannon, bought the tavern in 1876 for a summer home, retaining the name, South Mountain House. She was shocked by the "corruption" of Christian doctrine among the people of South Mountain. She exposed their corrupted beliefs and described their poverty-stricken lives in a book published in 1882. For her missionary work among them, she built the Gothic stone chapel that overlooks the Trail. Restored by Mr. Griffin, 1963-5, the chapel is open on Saturdays, Sundays, and holidays from 1 to 5 p.m.

The Sisters of St. Mary's of Notre Dame used the South Mountain House for a summer retreat from 1922 until 1925, when the property was again sold for commercial purposes. A dancing pavilion was added where the veranda is now located, and at one time "the tavern served as a full-blown brothel." Mitchell H. Dodson purchased the property in 1957. The stucco was removed from the stone facings, and the original fireplaces were uncovered.

Mason and Dixon Line

The Mason and Dixon Line, the boundary between Maryland and Pennsylvania, should not be overlooked. During the summer of 1765, Charles Mason and Jeremiah Dixon, British astronomers and surveyors, crossed with a small army of chainbearers, local surveyors, axmen, rodmen, cooks, and other laborers. A supporting road westward was constructed to transport supplies and equipment.

The boundary had been in dispute since the grant was made to William Penn in 1681. Lord Baltimore's colonists called the Pennsylvanians "Quaking Cowards," and the latter referred to the Catholics of Maryland as the "Hominy Gentry." The descendants of William Penn and George Calvert, the first Lord Baltimore, agreed to abide by a line that would be surveyed by the two reputable scientists, Mason and Dixon, who were then observing the transit of the planet Venus from a position in Africa. At the time of the survey, a line separating slave-holding colonies from the north was not contemplated, although it came to pass that Dixie, or Dixieland, became the name for the area south of the Mason and Dixon Line.

To mark the boundary line between the two colonies, milestones and, at five-mile intervals, crownstones were placed. Milestone No. 91 is the closest to the Appalachian Trail, but it is inaccesibly located on private land in Pen Mar. A nearby crownstone is No. 90, one mile east (as the crow flies), in the village of Highfield. These stones are made of limestone and were transported from England to the land underlain with limestone.

Industry

Whiskey making was perhaps the first industry along the Trail in Maryland. With the many sources of spring water on the slopes of South Mountain, corn, rye, and wheat grown in the valleys were made into whiskey, which was cheaper to ship to market then the bulkier grain. When a Federal tax was placed on whiskey in 1794, the distillers of South Mountain joined their compatriots in western Pennsylvania in the Whiskey Rebellion. A march on Frederick disbanded when the rebels learned that 500 Federal troops were waiting for them there.

Whiskey distilling continued into the late 1800s at Smithsburg on the northwest slope of South Mountain and at Burkittsville on the east slope of Crampton Gap. At Burkittsville in the 1880s, the Needwood Distillery (Golden Gate Whiskey) and Ahalt's Distillery were competitors. Both advertised using spring water from South Mountain. For aging and a better flavor, J. D. Ahalt shipped his whiskey to Rio de Janiero and back. Outerbridge Horsey made a better arrangement. After aging in his 3,000-barrel brick warehouse, his Golden Gate whiskey was shipped around the Horn to San Francisco for storage for a year before it was returned to Burkittsville, where it was again aged before sale.

Moonshining along the lower end of South Mountain and adjacent ridges of the Blue Ridge reached an advanced stage during Prohibition, when Spencer Weaver organized the moonshiners into a syndicate for production and marketing. Inducements for moonshiners to join his syndicate included a steady income and "cradle to the grave" fringe benefits.

Moonshiners were paid a monthly salary plus a production incentive based upon a unit price for whiskey delivered. If the occupational hazard of a raid resulted in a jail term for the moonshiner, the salary continued, and loans for capital equipment, repayable from later production proceeds, were made available for the re-establishment of the moonshiner in business.

Weaver provided a widow's pension in the event of an accidental death of the moonshiner, and he also had a standing arrangement with a funeral home in Harpers Ferry to cover burial costs. Spencer Weaver used the former Salty Dog Saloon across the Potomac from Harpers Ferry for the base of his operations. But prosperity may have ruined Weaver; he started drinking his own product, and mild heart attacks followed. One night he backed his auto into the C&O Canal and was found dead.

Iron-making became an important industry near South Mountain, where there were trees to burn for charcoal. The Frederick Forge of the 1750s became the Antietam Ironworks after Washington County was formed from Frederick in 1776. Catoctin Furnace was located to the northeast, Mount Aetna to the northwest, Keep Tryst near Harpers Ferry, and the Blue Ridge Ironworks at Knoxville. The installations at Harpers Ferry were heavy consumers of charcoal.

The effects of the iron furnaces on South Mountain were twofold. First, they provided employment for charcoal burners on South Mountain, and second, the denuding of the slopes by burning the hardwoods for charcoal caused erosion and contributed to the floods of the Potomac in the 19th century. A tannery, which operated for approximately 100 years at Burkittsville, also contributed to the erosion by buying tanbark stripped from chestnut and oak trees. Some of the charcoal burners remained behind on the mountain, eking out a meager existence into the 20th century.

Weverton was an unsuccessful industrial town despite its natural advantages. Casper W. Wever, after a successful career as a highway and railroad construction engineer, used his savings to purchase land and water rights and construct industrial buildings to found the town of Weverton. Wever favored the railroad over the canal and opposed a right-of-way through his property for the canal company. (When most of his buildings lay idle, he refused to lease space for a temporary hospital for canal workers who had contracted Asiatic cholera in the epidemic of 1833.) Wever believed that the drop of 15 feet in the Potomac above Weverton was sufficient to provide water power to turn 300,000 textile spindles (one source estimated 600,000). In 1834 he started construction on industrial buildings for leasing and on a diagonal dam across the Potomac for diverting water into his millrace to provide power for the buildings.

It was reported that Wever's lease charges were too high and the buildings were not constructed to meet the specifications of small factories. Only two buildings were leased, one for marble cutting and the other by a company that made files for the national armory in Harpers Ferry. The Weverton enterprise failed before the Civil War.

The springs at Weverton have always been important to the community. Scharf refers to a hotel at Weverton built in 1796, which burned before 1880, and which was one of the first hotels in the country to offer rooms with running water for ladies and gentlemen. The replacement hotel built in 1880 also had running water. The sons of the last owner, Harry G. Traver, remember that the water was piped from the spring down the hill to the hotel, and that the water was used to cool beer and watermelon in the hotel, which then catered to railroad workers. The hotel site was where Md 67 connected with US 340 before the 1964-65 relocation. The hotel was razed for the road construction in 1916.

Weverton has been without industry since the Trail was built, and even the railroad station, where steam locomotives puffed on the siding while taking on water, was dismantled during World War II.

The Chesapeake and Ohio Canal is now a historical park administered by the National Park Service. Intersecting the Appalachian Trail, it provides a comparatively level path along the Potomac for 184.5 miles from Washington to Cumberland. Operation came to an end in 1924 when a flood damaged its structures. It had operated at a loss for many years, and the low traffic did not warrant sizable new capital expenditures for repairs and improvements.

Civil War and Memorial Arch to War Correspondents

More words have been devoted to South Mountain during the Civil War than any other subject along the *AT* in Maryland. In addition, metal tablets in Turners and Crampton gaps provide details on troop movements during the Battle of South Mountain. Briefly, the Battle of South Mountain, September 14, 1862, was the curtain raiser for the Battle of Antietam or Sharpsburg. Finding lost Orders No. 191 revealed to the Union Command General Lee's orders to split his army into four segments and the routes for the three task forces detailed to capture Harpers Ferry, by-passed by the Confederates in the northern invasion. Union forces, superior in number and equipment, moved slowly and met strong resistance from small Confederate holding forces entrenched where the *AT* crosses Turners, Fox, Crampton and Brownsville gaps.

The Confederate command post was in the South Mountain Inn at Turners Gap. The delay permitted the three task forces under Stonewall Jackson to capture Harpers Ferry and allowed the Confederates to regroup on the west side of Antietam Creek, where the two armies fought each other to a standstill. Three days of fighting, beginning on South Mountain, resulted in the highest casualty rate of the war.

A Civil War correspondent, George Alfred Townsend, returned to South Mountain after the war. In 1884, flush with the proceeds from his books of fiction and syndicated newspaper articles on the Washington scene (he was the Drew Pearson of the post-Civil War period), he bought Crampton Gap. There he constructed a home, a house for his wife, a hall, a library, a lodge, a guesthouse, servants' houses, stables and a tomb for himself, where he was not buried. He called his estate "Gathland," "Gath" being his nom de plume. The buildings, mostly constructed of stone, were vandalized and only a wing of Gath Hall has been restored. The arch, dedicated in 1896 as a memorial to Civil War correspondents and artists, survives intact.

The 50-foot high memorial dominates Crampton Gap and frames the Catoctin Valley. It faces toward two other battlefields, Gettysburg and Winchester. The arch contains many inscriptions, and mythological figures are recessed in the stonework.

The off-balance arch has been described as an architectural cross between a Moorish arch and the tower on an old Frederick fire company station. The Hagerstown version is that Townsend adapted his architecture from the front of the Antietam Fire Co. building across from the B&O Railroad Station (now demolished for a parking lot) in Hagerstown, where Townsend observed the off-balance arch while awaiting transportation to his estate.

The arch is under the administration of the National Park Service, while the Maryland Department of Natural Resources administers the surrounding 135 acres constituting Gathland State Park.

Monument to George Washington

The first monument to George Washington to be completed is on Monument Knob north of Turners Gap. The observatory, 30 feet high and constructed of native stone, is shaped like an old-fashioned cream bottle. Here gathered citizens from Boonsboro on July 4, 1827, "to spend the day at hard labor. An aged survivor of the Revolution delivered an address and at its conclusion a cold collation was spread," according to an early reporter. The people of the South Mountain area like ceremonies, and this monument and the one in Crampton Gap have been rededicated several times. Restored by the CCC in 1934-35, the monument is the focus of Washington Monument State Park, which has picnic facilities.

Resorts

A few resorts flourished along the Appalachian Trail in Maryland. The first Black Rock Hotel, believed to be built shortly after the Civil War, burned in 1880. After being rebuilt in 1907, the occupancy period was short. South Mountain Inn in Turners Gap advertised itself as a summer resort from 1852 to 1859 after the drop in traffic on the National Road.

The popularity of Pen Mar, near the Pennsylvania line, more than compensated for the lackluster of other resorts. At the turn of the century, the area supported seven hotels and about 100 boarding houses. A Lutheran picnic drew 15,000 to Pen Mar Park, and 5,000 was not an uncommon draw on a summer day, when it was known as the Coney Island of the Blue Ridge. Special trains with several sections were scheduled by the Western Maryland Railroad from both east and west. Families were encouraged to spend the summer at Pen Mar while the breadwinners commuted to Baltimore, Hagerstown, and Waynesboro, which was connected to Pen Mar by trolley. The Blue Mountain House, a rambling three-story frame structure, accommodating 400 overnight guests, featured 50-cent Sunday dinners. It was built in 1883 and burned in 1913.

The Western Maryland Railroad opened Pen Mar Park in 1878 to promote passenger traffic and supplement railway income. Promotional publicity for the park claimed the observatory on High Rock could hold 500 people on its three tiers. The amusement park was leased to other operators in 1928 when the railroad management found that nine out of ten patrons of the park came by auto and bus. Pen Mar Park continued to operate with declining business until gas rationing in 1943 forced it to close.

History of the Appalachian Trail in Maryland

The first trail use along the crest of South Mountain may have been as a route for fugitive slaves making their way north, a link in the Underground Railway. Five of John Brown's men made their way north along South Mountain after the abortive raid on Harpers Ferry. Among John Brown's effects were maps showing mountain forts, and some believe that his strategy may have included building crude forts along South Mountain to cover their retreat after the raid.

A continuous trail along the ridge was not in evidence when the Appalachian Trail was laid out and built across Maryland by members of the PATC. The Trail was marked, cleared and paint-blazed in the winter of 1931 and spring of 1932.

The original five open shelters on South Mountain were constructed in the 1938-41 period. Bear Spring Cabin was dedicated by the PATC on May 1, 1941. Members of the Mountain Club of Maryland, located in Baltimore, and the Maryland Appalachian Trail Club of Hagerstown assisted members of the PATC in locating sites and negotiating leases with the owners. The Civilian Conservation Corps provided labor and the PATC supplied materials and technical assistance in the construction.

Maryland's Department of Forests and Parks in the mid-1950s announced a plan to acquire land on South Mountain for watershed protection, including the practice of forestry and recreation. By 1964 approximately 4,000 acres had been acquired. The plan lay dormant during the ensuing five years with the exception of the development of the Greenbrier Park. Frederick County, during this period, classified most of the east slope in private ownership in a recreational category that barred new homes for permanent residences but excluded land uses existing at the time of rezoning.

In May 1970, Maryland became the second state to pass legislation to protect the Appalachian Trail. The bill (S.84) directed the state to acquire land for the purpose of protecting and maintaining the Trail across the state. The bill was introduced by State Senator Goodloe Byron of Frederick in January 1970, and was signed by Governor Mandel on May 5, 1970.

The proposed amendments to the National Trails System Act were introduced by two Maryland legislators (Rep. Goodloe E. Byron and Sen. Charles C. Mathias). Today, Maryland continues its land purchases under the Open Space Program of the Department of Natural Resources.

SELECTED REFERENCES

For a complete footnoted version of the preceding history, see the sixth edition. The following publications are among the principal sources:

Dahlgren, Madeline V., *South Mountain Magic* (Boston: James R. Osgood, 1882; Reprinted 1974, Washington Co. Public Library, Hagerstown, Md.).

Maryland Geological Survey, *Report on the Highways of Maryland* (Baltimore: Johns Hopkins University Press, 1889).

Maryland Geological Survey, *Report on the Resurvey of the Maryland-Pennsylvania Boundary* (Baltimore, 1908).

Salzberg, Michael, "Boonsboro Washington Monument," Washington Post, March 5, 1970.

Sanderlin, Walter S., *The Great National Project, A History of the Chesapeake and Ohio Canal* (Baltimore: Johns Hopkins University Press, 1946).

Scharf, Thomas J., *A History of Western Maryland* (Philadelphia: Louis H. Everts, 1882).

Schletterbeck, Judy, *The Pen Mar Story* (privately published, 1977).

Williams, Thomas J.C., *A History of Washington County, Maryland* (Hagerstown: Runk and Titsworth, 1906), vol. 1.

Dahlgren Chapel–Turners Gap, Maryland   Rick Canter

AT Elevation Profile -- Maryland Section 1

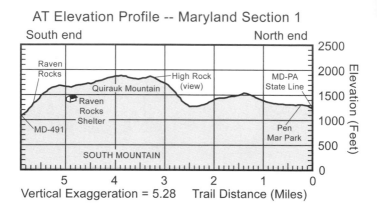

South end   North end

Raven
Rocks

Quirauk Mountain

High Rock
(view)

MD-PA
State Line

Raven
Rocks
Shelter

MD-491

Pen
Mar Park

SOUTH MOUNTAIN

Elevation (Feet)
2500
2000
1500
1000
500
0

5   4   3   2   1   0
Vertical Exaggeration = 5.28   Trail Distance (Miles)

Raven Rock Shelter   Henry Horn

SECTION 1
PEN MAR ROAD TO RAVEN ROCK HOLLOW
(MD 491)
Distance: 5.9 Miles

The partial ascent of Quirauk Mountain heading southbound is the most strenuous on the *AT* in Maryland. The main points of interest are Pen Mar County Park (see highlights) and High Rock, which offers an expansive view and is used as a launching point by hang gliders.

Road Access

Northern end of section at Pen Mar Road: From US 15, take Md 550 west. Turn right at a castle-like gate, onto McAfee Hill Rd, then left onto Pen Mar Rd. At beginning of Pen Mar County Park, turn right (still on Pen Mar Rd). (To reach Pen Mar Park, continue straight ahead.) Cross into Pennsylvania and over railroad tracks. The *AT* crossing of Pen Mar Rd (NAD83 N39° 43.253', W77° 30.422') is 90 yd beyond the tracks. There is room for two cars to park on the right side of the gate here. Do not block gate. Distance is 71 mi from Washington, D.C.

From I-81, take Pa 16 east to Rouzerville, Pennsylvania. In Rouzerville, turn right onto Pen Mar Rd. The *AT* crosses Pen Mar Rd 90 yd before a bridge over railroad tracks. See above. Distance is 4.0 mi from Waynesboro.

Southern end of section at Raven Rock Hollow: From I-70, take Md 66 north. Turn right onto Md 64 and right onto Md 491 (Raven Rock Road). The *AT* crosses Md 491 (NAD83 N39° 39.875', W77° 32.158') at the western end of a guardrail 0.2 mi before you reach the intersection of Ritchie Rd. There is room for cars to park on the shoulder of Md 491. Distance is 2.8 mi from Smithsburg.

From US 15, take Md 77 west. Turn right onto Md 64, then see above.

Maps

PATC Map 5 and USGS Smithsburg Quadrangle.

Shelters, Campsites, and Other Public Facilities

Raven Rock Shelter and nearby spring at 4.9/1.0.

Pen Mar County Park is 0.2 mi south of the northern end of this section. Camping is not permitted, but water and restrooms are available April through October. There is a pay telephone inside the visitor center. There is parking for day use only (April–October). Overnight parking is permitted in the large gravel lot across the Pen Mar-High Rock Road. A parking permit is required for the overnight lot. Call 240-313-2700 to secure an overnight lot permit.

Rouzerville, Pennsylvania, with stores, is 2.0 mi to the west on Pen Mar Rd.

Water and Supplies

Water is available at Pen Mar County Park (April–October) and near the shelter at 4.9/1.0 (reach *spring* by following trail leading east 0.3. mi).

Crampton Gap Shelter   John McDowell

SECTION HIGHLIGHTS

Mason-Dixon line – Now serving as the border between Maryland and Pennsylvania, the Mason-Dixon line was surveyed in 1765 to resolve a dispute between Britain and the American colonies. Crown stones were placed along the line at regular intervals (none are visible today from the *AT*).

Pen Mar County Park – The Western Maryland Railroad established Pen Mar Park on this site in 1877. The railroad operated the park until 1943. Park attractions included a roller coaster, movie theater, carousel, miniature train, photo studio, and a dance pavilion. A dining hall seated 450 people and offered dinners for $0.50. The dance pavilion still exists and features live big-band music each Sunday during the summer. Plaques mark the former locations of the other attractions. Camping is not permitted, but water and restrooms are available in season. An overlook shelter provides expansive westward views. There is a pay telephone inside the visitor center. Overnight parking is permitted in the gravel lot across the Pen Mar-High Rock Road from the park entrance. A permit is required.

Large mound to the east, with 3-ft high stone wall on Trail side, encloses a deep pit, probably an artificial pond at one time. There are many vestiges of former habitation in this vicinity. About 100 yd north of the mound: 20 ft to west are ruins of stone-lined root cellar; 50 ft to west are ruins of brick-lined, cellar foundation.

N-S	TRAIL DESCRIPTION	

0.0 Northern end of section at Pennsylvania state line and   **5.9**
Pen Mar Rd (**Mason-Dixon line**). Southbound: From
Pen Mar Rd pass over *AT* corridor gate. Continue
south on trail 100 yd, turn east and cross railroad tracks
onto gravel lane heading uphill. After 20 yd, turn west
and continue past gate. Northbound: To continue on
Trail, cross Pen Mar Rd, into Pennsylvania.

0.2 Southbound: Enter grassy area of **Pen Mar County**   **5.7**
Park. Continue straight ahead, passing overlook shelter
on west and dance pavilion on east. Northbound:
Exit grassy area of Pen Mark County Park, and pass
gate. About 30 yd beyond gate, turn west onto gravel
lane and cross railroad tracks. Continue downhill 90
yd, then turn east to Pen Mar Rd.

0.3 Southbound: Exit grassy area of Pen Mar County   **5.6**
Park, and enter woods. Northbound: Enter grassy area
of Pen Mar County Park. Continue straight ahead,
passing dance pavilion on east and overlook shelter
on west.

0.5 Southbound: Turn east, climbing embankment, and   **5.4**
in 40 yd turn west onto old forest road. Northbound:
Turn west descending and in 40 yd turn east on old
road.

0.9 Cross unused forest road (which leads east 0.3 mi to   **5.0**
paved High Rock Rd).

1.1 **Large mound** and stone wall on east.   **4.8**

1.2 Cross clearing for buried cable (leads 0.1 mi east to   **4.7**
gated, paved High Rock Rd).

1.3 Cross unused forest road which leads 0.16 mi east to   **4.6**
gated, paved High Rock Rd.

High Rock Loop Trail - Leads 0.1 mi to High Rock and a parking lot. High Rock has a spectacular view and is a popular hang-gliding site. Stone foundations and a modern cement platform mark site of former 30-ft high pavilion. Paved High Rock Rd leads 1.7 mi directly down to Pen Mar County Park. There is room for 15 cars to park in immediate area of High Rock.

Quirauk Mtn - The partial ascent of Quirauk Mtn southbound starting at 2.6 is the most strenuous on the *AT* in Maryland.

Raven Rock Shelter – Shelter is 0.1 mi west of *AT*. Spring is reached by descending 200 ft along a trail that leads east from *AT* for 0.3 mi. Unblazed trail beyond spring leads 0.1 mi to Devils Racecourse, a remarkable boulder field, and another 0.1 mi to Ritchie Road. The Raven Rock Shelter spring runs strong until mid-summer then slowly dries up; but there is another spring higher up 30 ft downhill from the trail that runs well all season. Accessible straight downhill, off trail, about 15 ft before first switchback ascending.

N-S	TRAIL DESCRIPTION	
1.5	Cross unused forest road (leads 0.15 mi east to gated, paved High Rock Rd). *Southbound*: Expect trail to get rocky. Follow blazes carefully.	**4.4**
2.6	Trail passes between two boulders. *Southbound*: Trail ascends across steep rock fields over next 0.5 mi. *Northbound*: Expect rocky going. Follow blazes carefully.	**3.3**
3.1	Western end of blue-blazed **High Rock Loop Trail** enters from east.	**2.8**
3.2	Eastern end of blue-blazed **High Rock Loop Trail** enters from east.	**2.7**
3.9	Local high point on southwestern slope of **Quirauk Mtn.**	**2.0**
4.6	Dense undergrowth area (north) meets open forest area (south).	**1.3**
4.9	Junction with blue blazed **Raven Rock Shelter** trail to west and, to east, blue-blazed trail to spring.	**1.0**
5.7	At switchback turning west, a side trail leads 40 yd east to view atop Raven Rock cliff.	**0.2**
5.9	Southern end of section at Md 491, at western end of guardrail, in Raven Rock Hollow. Exercise extreme caution crossing highway! Ritchie Rd. and Md 491 intersect 0.2 mi to east. Southbound: From south side of road, follow path east along back side of guardrail.	**0.0**

AT Elevation Profile -- Maryland Section 2

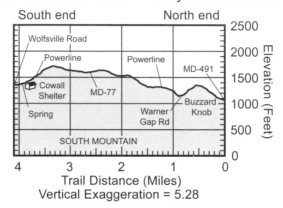

Which way to Katahdin?   Larry Broadwell

SECTION 2
RAVEN ROCK HOLLOW TO
WOLFSVILLE ROAD
Distance: 4.1 Miles

This section is geographically interesting in that it crosses two small ridges that form a curious, right-angle interruption in the South Mountain range. These ridges extend southeastward and link with the Catoctin range. The excellent footing will come as a relief after either adjoining section.

Road Access

Northern end of section at Raven Rock Hollow: From I-70, take Md 66 north. Turn right onto Md 64 and right onto Md 491 (Raven Rock Rd). The *AT* crosses Md 491 (NAD83 N39° 39.875', W77° 32.158') at the western end of a guardrail, 0.2 mi before you reach the intersection of Ritchie Rd. There is room for cars to park on the shoulder of Md 491.

From US 15, take Md 77 west. Turn right onto Md 64, then see above.

Southern end of section at Wolfsville Rd: From the east, on I-70 take the Md 17 Myersville-Middletown exit, and proceed north on Md 17 for 11.6 mi to a gravel lane on the right side of Md 17, which is now 11405 Wolfsville Rd. The lane has two entrances, which merge into one lane. Park along the sides of the lane. A blue-blazed trail, running parallel to Wolfsville Rd leads from the parking area north to *AT* (NAD83 N39° 37.806', W77° 33.542').

From the west, on I-70, take Md 66 north to Md 77 east. Turn right onto Md 77 and then right on Wolfsville Rd. Proceed uphill 1.4 mi to 11405 Wolfsville Rd and the gravel parking area on left (see above).

Alternate access at Warner Gap Rd: This gravel road leads one mi east from Md 491 to the *AT* (NAD83 N39° 39.345', W77° 32.307'). There is room for a few cars to park on shoulder at several places between stream crossing and *AT* crossing.

Alternate access at Foxville Rd (Md 77): There is shoulder parking where this road crosses the *AT* (NAD83 N39° 38.225', W77° 32.492'). Distances are 2.2 mi west to Md 64 near Smithsburg, and 8.8 mi east to US 15 near Thurmont.

Maps
PATC Map 5 and USGS Smithsburg Quadrangle.

Shelters, Campsites, and Other Public Facilities
Ensign Phillip Cowall Memorial Shelter, reached by a blue-blazed trail at 3.9/0.2 mi. Camping and open fires are prohibited in this section.

Free State Hostel is open for the long-distance backpacking public. This is located on Wolfsville Road north (downhill) from the Appalachian Trail 0.3 mi. Look for the "Free State" mailbox on the left (west) side of the road.

Water and Supplies
Water is available from *springs* at 0.9/3.2 mi and near Cowall Shelter, accessible by blue-blazed trail at 4.0/0.1 mi.

SECTION HIGHLIGHTS

Stone wall – Most of the stone walls that can be seen from the trail in this area were constructed long ago by farmers clearing their fields for planting. Trees have replaced the fields now, but the walls remain.

N-S	TRAIL DESCRIPTION	
0.0	Northern end of section begins at Md 491 (Raven Rock Rd) at western end of guardrail, 0.2 mi downhill from intersection of Ritchie Rd. Southbound: From south side of road, follow path east along back side of guardrail. Northbound: To continue on Trail, at end of guardrail, cross Md 491 diagonally to east and reenter woods, ascending steeply.	**4.1**
0.1	Cross Little Antietam Creek as it flows down through Raven Rock Hollow. Northbound: Turn west and follow guardrail.	**4.0**
0.4	Cross **stone wall**.	**3.7**
0.5	Reach local high point at gap on east slope of Buzzard Knob.	**3.6**
0.8	Warner Gap Rd. Southbound: Turn east onto gravel Warner Gap Rd. In 40 yd turn west off road. Northbound: Turn west on Warner Gap Rd. In 40 yd turn east off road and ascend into woods.	**3.3**
0.85	Cross Edgemont Reservoir feeder stream.	**3.25**
0.9	*Spring* is 10 ft west of trail	**3.2**
1.2	Cross clearing for powerline (no view).	**2.9**
1.9	Ascend/descend stone steps.	**2.4**
1.8	South end of 15 ft long rock outcrop.	**2.3**
2.1	Cross stream.	**2.0**
2.4	Local high point.	**1.7**
2.5	Woods (north) meet field (south).	**1.6**
2.6	Cross Md 77 (Foxville Rd).	**1.5**

SECTION HIGHLIGHTS

Cowall Shelter – Features a large sleeping area with additional space available on a second-floor balcony. The *spring* is reached by returning to the *AT* on the blue-blazed trail, then proceeding south 0.1 mi on *AT* to a blue-blazed trail heading east 40 yd to *spring*, excellent year round.

The shelter was built by students from Gallaudet University and Model Secondary School for the Deaf in Washington, D.C. with the help of PATC volunteers. It was constructed 20 miles away using a truckload of loblolly pine logs that were donated. When completed it was moved to its present site.

Corwall Shelter   John McDowell

N-S	TRAIL DESCRIPTION	
2.8	Woods (north) meet field (south).	**1.3**
2.9	Cross treeline between fields.	**1.2**
3.1	Field (north) meets woods (south).	**1.0**
3.7	Powerline clearing.	**0.4**
3.75	Pass house to east, owned by Maryland Department of Natural Resources.	**0.35**
3.9	**Cowall Shelter.** Blue-blazed trail descends 40 yd west to shelter.	**0.2**
4.0	Blue-blazed trail leads 0.1 mi east 40 yd to *spring*.	**0.1**
4.1	Blue-blazed trail leads left 400 ft to trailhead parking for 8 vehicles at 11405 Wolfsville Road. This turnoff is 10 ft before pavement of Wolfsville Road crossing.	**0.0**
4.1	Southern end of section at Wolfsville Rd. Southbound: To continue on Trail, cross road.	**0.0**

AT Elevation Profile -- Maryland Section 3

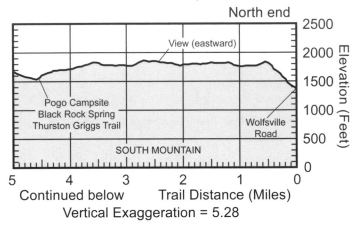

North end

Vertical Exaggeration = 5.28

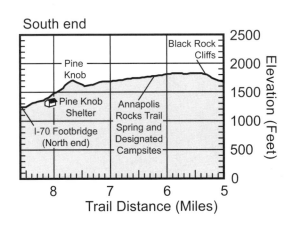

SECTION 3
WOLFSVILLE ROAD TO INTERSTATE 70
Distance: 8.6 Miles

This section presents a typical example of the narrow ridge crest peculiar to Maryland. The Trail is smooth except for a couple of rocky or rutted segments. The southern half is easier and has the main points of interest, which include expansive views from Black Rock and Annapolis Rock. The predominant growth is oak and hickory.

Road Access

Northern end of section at Wolfsville Road: From the east, on I-70 take the Md 17 Myersville-Middletown exit, and proceed north on Md 17 for 11.6 mi to a gravel lane on the right side of Md 17, at 11405 Wolfsville Rd. The lane has two entrances, which merge into one lane. Park along the sides of the lane. A blue-blazed trail, running parallel to Wolfsville Rd, leads from the parking area north to *AT* (NAD83 N39° 37.806', W77° 33.542').

From the west, on I-70, take Md 66 north to Md 77. Turn right onto Md 77 and then right on Wolfsville Rd, to the parking area on left at 11405 Wolfsville Rd. (see above).

Southern end of section at US 40: From the east, on I-70, take MD 17 exit 42, north into Myersville. Turn right to stay on Md 17, in the center of Myersville, then turn left onto US 40 westbound. Proceed 3 miles. There is a parking area (NAD83 N39° 32.127', W77° 36.224') on left after Canada Hill Road and before an I-70 overpass. Do not block private drives. From the parking area, cross the embankment at a large *AT* sign and follow a closed section of old highway. At end of old highway, before reaching a guardrail, take a blue-blazed trail left and descend to footbridge over I-70. Distance is 0.1 mi from parking area. *AT* southbound crosses footbridge. *AT* northbound does not cross footbridge, proceeds to right of footbridge, paralleling I-70 fenceline.

From the west, on I-70 take the US 40 east exit, east of Hagerstown. Cross I-70 overpass to parking area on right immediately after overpass. Then see directions above.

Maps
PATC Map 5 and USGS Smithsburg and Myersville Quadrangles.

Shelters, Campsites, and Other Public Facilities
Free State Hostel is available for the long-distance backpacking public 0.3 mi north of the Trail along Wolfsville Rd. From the *AT*, go downhill (NW) on the road and find "Free State" mailbox on left side.

Pogo Memorial Campsite (at 4.8/3.8 mi), with nearby *spring* and a privy.

A number of primitive campsites may be found near Annapolis Rock, which is reached by a blue-blazed trail descending sharply west from *AT* at 6.4/2.2 mi. A second blue-blazed trail leads 0.2 mi downhill from the campsite to a *spring*. No fires are allowed at Annapolis Rock.

Pine Knob Shelter (0.1 mi by either of two side trails, at 8.0/0.6 mi or 8.1/0/5 mi), with nearby *spring*.

A restaurant and phone are opposite the entrance to Greenbrier State Park, 0.5 mi west of the US 40 parking area. A bulletin board and display map are at the US 40 parking area.

Water and Supplies
Water is available from a spring on the blue-blazed Thurston Griggs Trail 300 ft west of Pogo Memorial Campsite (at 4.8/3.8 mi), Annapolis Rock (0.2 mi down side trail, at 6.3/2.2 mi), and Pine Knob Shelter (0.1 mi down side trail, at 7.9/0.5 mi).

Tammy McCorkle

Greenbriar Lake from Annapolis Rock

Old road – Descends steeply eastward to junction of Loy-Wolfe Rd and Black Rock Rd in 0.9 mi. Bottom 0.2 mi is on private land.

Pogo Memorial Campsite – Established on the site of the former Black Rock Hotel by the Mountain Club of Maryland as a memorial to its late member, Walter "Pogo" Rheinheimer, Jr. (1958-1974). Its use is free, on a first-come, first-served basis. The campground has a privy and two nearby *springs*, one accessible via a blue-blazed Thurston Griggs Trail that leads 70 yd down to main *spring*, on right. A smaller *spring* may be found in camp area to west of *AT*. The hillside *spring* is the only one reliable year round. (Do not use early season water at *AT* itself.) Camping is allowed on both sides of Trail; open fires are permitted only within established fire rings.

Thurston Griggs Trail descends 1.0 mi to trailhead parking at end of White Oak Rd, a residential public road off Crystal Falls Rd.

Black Rock Cliffs – Has a 180-degree westward view that is the best in this section.

Annapolis Rock – Includes an overhanging cliff with an excellent westward view that encompasses Greenbrier Lake. Near the cliff area are a number of primitive campsites. In campsite area, to left from access spur, blue-blazed trail leads 0.2 mi and 40 ft downhill to *spring* in small draw. This spring is the most reliable along the Maryland *AT*.

N-S	TRAIL DESCRIPTION	
0.0	Section starts on west side of Wolfsville Rd (Md 17).	**8.6**
0.6	Reach crest of ridge, with steep and rocky ascent/descent on both sides.	**8.0**
2.1	Northern end of area of extremely rocky footing as Trail follows eroded crest of South Mountain.	**6.5**
2.4	Good eastward view from talus slope on east.	**6.2**
3.1	Southern end of area of extremely rocky footing as Trail follows eroded crest of South Mountain.	**5.5**
3.8	Continue past forest road to west.	**4.8**
4.0	Reach junction with **old road** descending east.	**4.6**
4.2	Continue past forest road descending east.	**4.4**
4.7	Turn west off rutted road. Continue past forest road heading west.	**3.9**
4.8	Enter **Pogo Memorial Campsite** area. To stay on Trail, go straight at junction with blue-blazed **Thurston Griggs Trail**, descending west.	**3.8**
4.9	Cross intermittent Black Rock Creek.	**3.7**
5.4	Blue-blazed trails lead west 40 yd to **Black Rock Cliffs**. Note considerable scree at foot of cliff.	**3.2**
6.4	Blue-blazed trail descends sharply west 0.2 mi to **Annapolis Rocks**.	**2.2**
7.6	Reach local high point at slight saddle of ridge. Peak of Pine Knob is to east. Patches of cinnamon ferns, with their "fruity" summertime aroma, carpet both sides of Trail between 7.6/1.0 and 6.4/2.2 mi.	**1.0**

SECTION HIGHLIGHTS

Pine Knob Shelter – Water available at *spring*. Not dependable. Sometimes comes late and disappears in September. There are numerous good campsites near shelter.

Black Rock Cliffs

Isaac Wiegmann

N-S

TRAIL DESCRIPTION

8.0 Blue-blazed trail on west leads 0.1 mi to **Pine Knob Shelter**. Northbound: Steep, rutted ascent ahead. **0.6**

8.1 Blue-blazed trail to **Pine Knob Shelter** comes in from west **0.5**

8.2 Cross telephone line. **0.4**

8.4 Pass grassy woods road to east. **0.2**

8.5 Pass under US 40 overpass of I-70. Southbound: Continue on path paralleling I-70. Northbound: Ascend into woods. **0.1**

8.6 Southern end of section at footbridge that crosses I-70. Blue-blazed trail leads from bridge 0.1 mi to large parking lot on US 40. Southbound: To continue on Trail, at southern end of footbridge, go up stairs, then walk on Trail easement between two houses. Northbound: Turn east, (compass north) at northern end of footbridge, and parallel I-70 fenceline. **0.0**

S-N

AT Elevation Profile -- Maryland Section 4

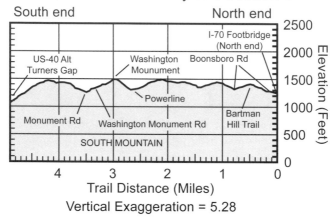

South end · North end

I-70 Footbridge (North end)

US-40 Alt Turners Gap

Washington Mounument

Boonsboro Rd

Powerline

Monument Rd · Washington Monument Rd

Bartman Hill Trail

SOUTH MOUNTAIN

Elevation (Feet): 2500 2000 1500 1000 500 0

Trail Distance (Miles): 4 3 2 1 0

Vertical Exaggeration = 5.28

I-70 bridge   Bill Cooke

SECTION 4
INTERSTATE 70 TO TURNERS GAP
Distance: 4.9 Miles

This easy section crosses a succession of low hills and includes access to a lake and a historic monument with a good view.

Road Access

Northern end of section at I-70: From the east, on I-70, take MD 17, exit 42, north into Myersville. Turn right to stay on Md 17, in the center of Myersville, then turn left onto US 40 west bound. Proceed 3 mi. There is a parking area (NAD83 N39° 32.127', W77° 36.224') on left after Canada Hill Road and before an I-70 overpass. Do not block private drives. From the parking area, cross the embankment at a large *AT* sign and follow a closed section of old highway. At end of old highway, before reaching a guardrail, take a blue-blazed trail left and descend steeply to footbridge over I-70. Distance is 0.1 mi from parking area. *AT* southbound crosses footbridge. *AT* northbound proceeds to right of footbridge, paralleling I-70 fenceline.

From the west, on I-70 take the US 40 east exit, east of Hagerstown. Proceed on US 40 eastbound for 5.6 mi. Cross I-70 overpass to parking area on right immediately after overpass. Then see directions above.

Southern end of section at Turners Gap: From the east, on I-70, take exit 48, US Alt-40 west. Proceed west through Braddock Heights and Middletown, for 8 mi. Find the Old South Mountain Inn on left. Park at the east end of the Old South Mountain Inn parking lot (NAD83 N39° 29.065', W77° 37.172'). Find the *AT* on the north-east edge of the parking lot, near Alt. 40. Distance is 57 miles from Washington, D.C.

From the west, US Alt-40 diverges from US 40 just outside of Hagerstown, but has no junction with I-70. US Alt-40 may also be reached, from I-81, via Md 68; or from Shepherdstown via Md 34. Then see above. Distance is 2 miles from Boonsboro.

From US 340, take Md 67 north and turn right onto US Alt-40. Then see above.

Alternate access at Washington Monument State Park: From US Alt-40 at Turners Gap, turn north onto Washington Monument Rd. Cross Zittlestown Rd and enter park (NAD83 N39° 29.824', W77° 37.200'). Hiker parking is free, but the entrance gate is locked at night. It is open 8:00 a.m. to sunset every day. Youth group camping may be arranged by lower parking lot.

Maps
PATC Map 5/6, and USGS Myersville and Middletown Quadrangles.

Shelters, Campsites, and Other Public Facilities
Washington Monument State Park allows camping for youth groups only. The park also has a telephone, restrooms, and *water*. Write to Superintendent, Washington Monument State Park, Route 1, Middletown, MD or call 301-432-8065. Camping and fires are prohibited everywhere else in this section.

Greenbrier State Park, with access via a blue-blazed trail (0.5/4.4 mi) offers *water* and seasonal campsites, including the use of restrooms with shower, for a fee of $25 per night. There also is a shower facility and a camp store in the beach area.

Old South Mountain Inn (at Turners Gap) provides meals, but not lodging.

Water and Supplies
Boonsboro (2 miles west of Turners Gap) has grocery and hardware stores and a post office. *Water* and restrooms are available at Washington Monument State Park (at 3.1/1.8 mi) and at Greenbrier State Park (0.5/4.4 mi).

Washington Monument   John McDowell

Greenbrier State Park has a 42-acre, man-made lake and beach for swimming, boating and fishing. There are picnic tables, grills, boat rentals and a camp store. There are 165 campsites and bath houses with hot showers. For reservations call 1-888-432-2267. Pets are not allowed in the developed areas.

Washington Monument in Washington Monument State Park – First completed monument to George Washington, built in 1827, and restored by the CCC between 1934 and 1936. Interior stairs lead to a spectacular view from the top of monument; if tower is locked, view from ground level is still best view along this section. In the spring and fall, bird watchers flock to the top of the monument to sight migrating hawks, eagles, and ospreys as they soar along the mountain ridge.

N-S

TRAIL DESCRIPTION

0.0	Northern end of section at footbridge that crosses over I-70. Blue-blazed trail leads straight from bridge 0.1 mi to large parking lot on US 40. Southbound: Cross interstate footbridge. At southern end of footbridge, go up stairs, then walk on Trail easement between two houses. *Please stay on Trail.* Northbound: To continue on Trail, turn west (compass north) at northern end of footbridge and parallel I-70 fenceline.	**4.9**
0.1	Cross paved Boonsboro Mountain Rd. Southbound: Cross road diagonally to east and enter woods. Northbound: Cross road diagonally to west. Trail passes through easement between two houses. *Please stay on Trail.* Descend stairs and cross footbridge over I-70.	**4.8**
0.5	High point on Bartman Hill. Blue-blazed trail to west descends 0.6 mi to the Visitor Center at **Greenbrier State Park**.	**4.4**
0.8	Cross paved Boonsboro Mountain Rd.	**4.1**
0.9	Cross telephone line.	**4.0**
1.1	Reach local high point.	**3.8**
2.1	Unmarked path leads east short distance to rocks with good winter view.	**2.8**
2.6	Cross high-tension powerline clearing, then ascend.	**2.3**
2.8	Large talus slope with winter view to west. *Be careful of loose rocks.*	**2.1**
2.9	Junction with trail to **Washington Monument**, in Washington Monument State Park, 100 yd south. To continue on *AT*: Southbound, turn left. Northbound: turn right and descend.	**2.0**

S-N

SECTION HIGHLIGHTS

Washington Monument State Park – In addition to the Washington Monument, the complex includes a museum, restrooms, a public phone, and ranger residence. *Water* is available from an all-season trailside water tap between the Mt. Vernon Shelter and upper parking lot.

Turners Gap – Old South Mountain Inn is located west of the *AT*, on the south side of Alt-40. Used by several Presidents, the inn is at least 200 years old. It is one of the oldest public houses along the *AT*. Opposite the inn is **Dahlgren Chapel**, a Gothic stone building. The chapel was built by the widow of Admiral Dahlgren, inventor of the Dahlgren naval cannon. Part of the Battle of South Mountain was fought in the vicinity of Turners Gap, but heavier fighting centered around Fox Gap.

N-S	TRAIL DESCRIPTION	
3.1	Cross park road in **Washington Monument State Park**. Southbound: Turn east on park road, passing "do not enter" sign, then turn west onto *AT* and proceed downhill. Northbound: Turn west on park road, then turn east onto *AT* at "foot trail to monument" sign and proceed uphill.	**1.8**
3.25	Cross **Washington Monument State Park** road leading to a hiker parking lot.	**1.65**
3.3	Cross **Washington Monument State Park** entrance road.	**1.6**
3.5	Cross Monument Rd.	**1.4**
4.0	Cross two stone fences 70 yd apart.	**0.9**
4.9	Southern end of section at US Alt-40, **Turners Gap**. Southbound: To continue on Trail, cross US Alt-40. Northbound: Ascend field to west of **Dahlgren Chapel**.	**0.0**

AT Elevation Profile -- Maryland Section 5

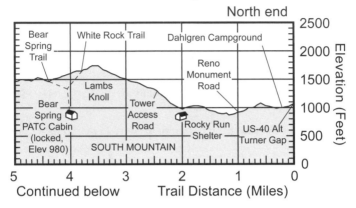

North end

Vertical Exaggeration = 5.28

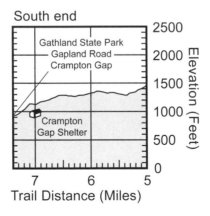

SECTION 5
TURNERS GAP TO CRAMPTON GAP
Distance: 7.4 Miles

This is a relatively easy section with genuinely excellent footing. The ascent of Lambs Knoll is steeper from the north.

Road Access
Northern end of section at Turners Gap: From the east, on I-70, take US Alt-40, exit 49, west. Take Alt-40 west for 9 mi. The *AT* crosses US Alt-40 just east of Old South Mountain. Parking is available in the southeast corner of the Old South Mountain Inn parking lot only (NAD83 N39° 29.065', W77° 37.172'). Follow signs for hikers.

From the west, US Alt-40 diverges from US 40 just outside of Hagerstown, but has no junction with I-70. US Alt-40 may also be reached from I-81, via Md 68; or from Sheperdstown via Md 34. Then see above. Distance is 2 miles from Boonsboro.

From US 340, take Md 67 north and turn right onto US Alt-40. Then see above.

Southern end of section at Gathland State Park in Crampton Gap (NAD83 N39° 24.342', W77° 38.384'): From US Alt-40, take Md 67 south (from west), or Md 17 south (from east). From MD 67 turn east onto Gapland Road; from MD 17 turn left on Main Street in Burkittsville. From US 340, take Md 67 north (from west), or Md 17 north (from east), and see above. The park has two free parking lots. The first lot is south of Gapland Road, at the end of the ascending park road. The second lot is north of Gapland Road, with access off Arnoldstown Road.

Alternate access at Reno Monument Rd: At Fox Gap there is parking south of Reno Monument Rd at the intersection with Lambs Knoll

Rd (NAD83 N39° 28.243', W77° 37.053'). Please do not park on the Appalachian Trail.

Maps

PATC Map 6 and USGS Middletown and Keedysville Quadrangles.

Shelters, Campsites, and Other Public Facilities

Camping is permitted only at the camping areas described below.

Dahlgren Back Pack Campground (at 0.2/7.2 mi), established and maintained by the Maryland Park Service, has numerous excellent sites, restrooms, water, and showers. Use is free on a first-come, first-served basis.

Rocky Run Shelter (0.2 mi by side trail, at 2.0/5.4 mi), accommodates five persons. Excellent year-round spring.

Crampton Gap Shelter (0.3 mi by side trail, at 7.0/0.4 mi, accommodates eight persons. Intermittent spring. All-season piped water at Park.

Bear Spring Cabin (0.5 mi by side trail, at 4.4/3.0 mi) is a locked cabin owned by the PATC. See "Shelters and Cabins."

Water and Supplies

Old South Mountain Inn (at Turners Gap) provides meals, but not lodging. Boonsboro (2 mi west of Turners Gap) has grocery and hardware stores and a post office. *Water* is available at Dahlgren Back Pack Campground (at 0.2/7.2 mi), from Bear Spring (0.3 mi by side trail, at 4.4/3.0 mi), and at Gathland State Park (hand pump beside closed restroom) in season.

Reno Monument at Fox Gap, along the AT on South Mountain   Larry Broadwell

Turners Gap - Old South Mountain Inn is located west of the *AT*, on the south side of Alt-40. Used by several Presidents, the inn is at least 200 years old. It is one of the oldest public houses along the *AT*. Opposite the inn is **Dahlgren Chapel**, a Gothic stone building. The chapel was built by the widow of Admiral Dahlgren, inventor of the Dahlgren naval cannon. Part of the Battle of South Mountain was fought in the vicinity of Turners Gap, but heavier fighting centered around Fox Gap.

Dahlgren Back Pack Campground – Operated by South Mountain State Park. *Water* (April-Oct), restrooms, and hot showers.

Fox Gap – Originally called "Fox's Gap," this area was the scene of heavy fighting during the Battle of South Mountain, Sept. 14, 1862. The Federal left flank, under Major General Reno, enveloped the Confederate right flank, under Brigadier General Garland, with the gap as the attack's focal point. Both Generals were killed in the battle, and Rutherford B. Hayes, a future President, was wounded. Reno Monument, erected by veterans of the 9th U.S. Army Corps on Sept. 14, 1998, is 50 yd to east. The monument honors the 17th Michigan Volunteer Infantry Regiment and General Burnside's 9th Army Corp. Various plaques describe the battle of South Mountain.

Paved road – This is a maintenance access road to complex of Lambs Knoll communications and FAA towers (to southwest) and Reno Monument Rd (to northeast).

Rocky Run Shelter – Accommodates five and has excellent year-round *spring*.

N-S

TRAIL DESCRIPTION

0.0	Northern end of section, at US Alt-40 near eastern edge of parking lot for Old South Mountain Inn, opposite **Dahlgren Chapel**, at **Turners Gap**. Southbound: *AT* enters woods parallel to dirt road for first 100 yd, descending slightly. Northbound: To continue on *AT*, cross US Alt-40 and ascend field on west side of chapel.	**7.4**
0.2	**Dahlgren Back Pack Campground** to west of Trail. Southbound: Just ahead, ascend on old road. Northbound: Ascend slightly, eventually paralleling to west of gravel road.	**7.2**
1.0	Cross paved Reno Monument Rd, at **Fox Gap**. Lambs Knoll Rd is to east of Trail. Southbound: Bear west through dirt parking lot and then through grassy field. Northbound: Cross dirt parking lot, turn north at Lambs Knoll Rd, cross Reno Monument Rd, and continue on *AT* past a plaque at edge of Reno Monument Rd.	**6.4**
1.1	Field. Southbound: Enter woods at edge of field. Northbound: Cross grassy field.	**6.3**
1.5	Cross high-tension powerline clearing. Westward view.	**5.9**
1.7	Old road. Southbound: Turn east. Northbound: Turn west and descend.	**5.7**
2.0	Blue-blazed trail on west side of *AT* descends 110 ft in 0.2 mi to **Rocky Run Shelter** and *spring*. Northbound: *AT* ascends for next 0.3 mi.	**5.4**
2.5	**Paved road**. Southbound: Bear slightly west and cross paved road. Northbound: Cross paved road, bearing slightly to east.	**4.9**

S-N

SECTION HIGHLIGHTS

White Rocks Trail – Descends 310 ft over 0.23 mi to intersect Bear Spring Cabin Trail midway between *AT* and *Bear Spring.* This side trail is rough, steep and not recommended for children. Bear Spring Cabin Trail then descends another 250 ft over another 0.21 mi to reach Bear Spring. Easier access from *AT* at 4.4/3.0 mi.

Bear Spring Cabin Trail descends to east, 360 ft in 0.5 mi, to *Bear Spring* and another 0.2 mi to PATC locked Bear Spring Cabin. See "*Shelters and Cabins.*" Highway is 0.35 beyond cabin.

Crampton Gap Shelter – First built in 1941 by the CCC. It accommodates eight persons. The *spring* runs faint in June-July, and usually dries by August.

Gathland State Park in Crampton Gap – On east, at fork of Arnoldtown and Gapland roads, is 50-ft tall stone memorial to Civil War newspaper correspondents, erected by George Alfred Townsend (a Civil War journalist who used the pen-name "Gath"). On hill to the south is Gath Hall, of the Townsend estate, which was restored as a museum in 1958. The park has a picnic pavilion in a field and an adjacent parking lot to the north of Gapland Road. Heavy fighting occurred in the field during the Battle of Crampton's Gap, Sept. 14, 1862. The Federals, under Franklin, eventually overwhelmed the greatly outnumbered Confederates, under McLaws.

Ruins of a large stone barn (circa 1887) are to the west of the Trail, north of the picnic pavilion. The Museum, Gath Hall, and restrooms for Gathland State Park, located on south side of Gapland Road, were closed for budgetary reasons in 1993. *Water* pump to left of restroom structure is seasonal.

N-S | TRAIL DESCRIPTION

3.6   High point near summit of Lambs Knoll. (Unblazed,   **3.8**
unmaintained trail to west leads 50 yd to fenced
communication tower on summit.)

3.8   White Rocks quartzite cliff on east offers an   **3.6**
impressive view south along the ridge that *AT*
traverses. "R.L. Rudy 1890" is carved into the rock
face. Blue-blazed **White Rocks Trail** intersects on
south side of Trail. Southbound: *AT* bears west.
Northbound: At cliff, *AT* bears west.

4.4   Junction of *AT* and blue-blazed **Bear Spring**   **3.0**
Cabin Trail, which comes in from east side of Trail.
Southbound: Turn right. Northbound: Bear left.

7.0   Blue-blazed trail leads east 0.25 mi to **Crampton**   **0.4**
Gap Shelter and intermittent *spring*.

7.3   **Gathland State Park,** north of Gapland Rd.   **0.1**
Southbound: Reach grassy area at Gathland State
Park, near ruins of large stone barn (circa 1887) on
west. Pass between parking lot on east and picnic
pavilion on west. Northbound: Cross grassy area,
passing between parking lot on east and pavilion on
west. Pass large stone barn (circa 1887) and enter
woods.

7.4   Southern end of section, in **Gathland State Park**,   **0.0**
at Gapland Rd. in Crampton Gap. Southbound:
Pass through gap in stone wall and reach Gapland
Rd. To continue on *AT*, ascend paved driveway in
park. Northbound: Pass through opening in stone
wall on north side of Gapland Rd, cross grassy area
with picnic pavilion on west and parking lot on east.
Ascend wooded hillside.

S-N

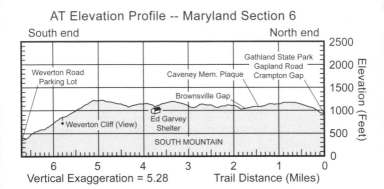

AT Elevation Profile -- Maryland Section 6

South end / North end

Weverton Road Parking Lot
Caveney Mem. Plaque
Gathland State Park
Gapland Road
Crampton Gap
Brownsville Gap
Weverton Cliff (View)
Ed Garvey Shelter
SOUTH MOUNTAIN

Elevation (Feet): 2500, 2000, 1500, 1000, 500, 0

Vertical Exaggeration = 5.28 / Trail Distance (Miles)

6 5 4 3 2 1 0

Memorial to Civil War newspaper correspondents © Van Hill

SECTION 6
CRAMPTON GAP TO WEVERTON
Distance: 6.7 Miles

The historical interest in Crampton Gap and the view from Weverton Cliffs make this one of the most popular sections of the *AT* in Maryland. The Trail follows the crest of both the narrow ridge and the western rim, with little change in elevation, through a mature forest with excellent footing. North to south is easier because there is a net descent of 570 feet between Crampton Gap and Weverton.

Road Access

Northern end of section at Gathland State Park in Crampton Gap (NAD83 N39° 24.342', W77° 38.384'): From US Alt-40, take Md 67 south (from west), or Md 17 south (from east). From MD 67 turn east onto Gapland Road; from MD 17 turn left on Main Street in Burkittsville. From US 340, take Md 67 north (from west), or Md 17 north (from east), and see above. The park has two free parking lots. The first lot is south of Gapland Road, at the end of the ascending park road. The second lot is north of Gapland Road, with access off Arnoldstown Road.

Southern end of section at Weverton: From US 340, take Md 67 north. Then take first right, turning onto Weverton Rd. On the right in 1500 ft is a Park and Ride lot (NAD83 N39° 19.977', W77° 40.997'). Trail access is at middle of parking area. From US Alt-40, follow Md 67 south approx. 12 mi (1.1 mi beyond Garrett Mill Rd on right). Do not take the Weverton Rd that is 0.3 mi north of Garrett Mill Rd. Turn left onto "Weverton Rd" (last intersection before reaching US 340). *AT* parking area is on the right.

Maps
PATC Map 6 and USGS Keedysville and Harpers Ferry Quadrangles.

Shelters, Campsites, and Other Public Facilities
Ed Garvey Shelter (at 3.7/3.0 mi). Otherwise, camping and fires are prohibited throughout this section. *Water* is available only at the spring near the Ed Garvey Shelter, and at Crampton Gap, in season. **Burkittsville** has a post office.

SECTION HIGHLIGHTS

Burkittsville – 1 mi east on Gapland Rd is an 1824 village that time seems to have forgotten. It has no amenities other than a post office, but is very charming.

Gathland State Park in Crampton Gap – Originally known as "Crampton's Gap." On east, at fork of Arnoldtown and Gapland rds, is a 50-ft tall stone memorial to Civil War newspaper correspondents, erected by George Alfred Townsend, a Civil War journalist who used the pen name "Gath." Museum for Gathland State Park lies in the gap. Midway up driveway, on east, is restroom building (closed) but *water* is available in season from hand pump at far end, by soda vending machine. At top of driveway, at far end of larger parking lot on west, inside surrounding stone fence line, is Townsend's empty stone mausoleum.

Unmarked side path – Leads a short distance to slight remnants of Civil War trenches. Heavy fighting occurred here during the Battle of Crampton's Gap, Sept. 14, 1862. The Federals, under Franklin, eventually overwhelmed the greatly outnumbered Confederates, under McLaws.

Memorial – Caveney helped maintain this section of Trail with his father. He was killed in an auto accident, and his father established a fund that was used to purchase a 4-acre tract surrounding the memorial, which was dedicated in March 1976.

N-S	TRAIL DESCRIPTION	

0.0 Northern end of section, at Gapland Rd in **Gathland State Park in Crampton Gap**. Southbound: Ascend park road south of Gapland Rd 0.1 mi to parking lot. Continue into woods at northeast corner of lot. Northbound: To continue on Trail, cross Gapland Rd and pass through opening in stone wall.   **6.7**

0.1 Intersection with **unmarked side path** to east.   **6.6**

1.4 Red granite **memorial** plaque to Glenn R. Caveney set flush with ground 10 ft to east of *AT*.   **5.3**

1.7 Cross remains of unmarked **Brownsville Gap** road.   **5.0**

3.7 Blue-blazed trail leads east 100 yd to **Ed Garvey Shelter** and *reliable spring* 0.4 mi. steeply downhill from shelter.   **3.0**

5.8 Blue-blazed trail, at bend in Trail, leads south 0.1 mi to **Weverton Cliffs**. Southbound: Follow bend to right. Ahead, Trail continues descent using 16 well-engineered switchbacks.   **0.9**

6.6 Southbound: Leave woods, cross Weverton Rd and continue ahead on *AT* along south side of Weverton Rd, on back side of guardrail. Northbound: Enter woods.   **0.1**

6.7 Southern end of section is adjacent to south side of *AT* Park and Ride lot on Weverton Rd. (Md 67 is 0.2 mi farther along Weverton Rd.) Southbound: To continue on Trail, follow blazes south from Park and Ride lot. Northbound: Turn east on *AT* near Park and Ride lot. Parallel Weverton Rd at foot of embankment, then cross Weverton Rd. Beside a telephone pole, enter woods and begin 480-ft ascent via 16 well-engineered switchbacks to spur leading to Weverton Cliffs.   **0.0**

SECTION HIGHLIGHTS

Brownsville Gap – In September 1862, two Confederate Army divisions crossed the mountain here on their way west to seize Maryland Heights, above Harpers Ferry.

Ed Garvey Shelter – Built in 2000 in memory of Ed Garvey, lifelong advocate for the Trail, life member of PATC, and author of *Appalachian Hiker: Adventure of a Lifetime*," written after his first thru-hike of the *AT* in 1970. His book served as a primary reference, how-to guide, and inspiration for hundreds of hikers in the 70s and 80s. The Garvey Shelter is one of the most recently-constructed shelters, with an upstairs sleeping loft and a balcony overlooking the main sleeping area. The *spring* is an excellent year-round water source.

Weverton Cliffs – Offer magnificent view of Potomac River gorge. Set in stone at the cliffs, 20 ft to right of Trail, is a plaque in memory of Congressman Goodloe E. Byron, 1928-78, a great supporter of the *AT*.

Bill Cooke

Ed Garvey Shelter

AT Elevation Profile -- Maryland Section 7

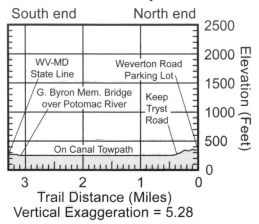

Harpers Ferry from Maryland Heights

Harpers Ferry from Maryland Heights   John McDowell

SECTION 7
WEVERTON TO HARPERS FERRY
Distance: 3.3 Miles

For most of this section, the Trail utilizes the towpath along the abandoned Chesapeake & Ohio Canal, a National Historical Park. The level terrain and excellent footing make it the easiest section in this book. The scenery, with the Potomac River on one side and the canal on the other, offers a pleasant change from the adjoining ridges.

Road Access

Northern end of section at Weverton: From US 340, take Md 67 north. Then take first right, turning onto Weverton Rd. In 1500 feet, on right is a Park and Ride parking area (NAD83 N39° 19.977', W77° 40.997'). Trail access is at middle of parking area. From US Alt-40, follow Md 67 south approx. 12 mi (1.1 mi beyond Garrett Mill Rd on right). Do not take the Weverton Rd that is 0.3 miles north on Garrett Mill Rd. Turn left onto "Weverton Rd" (last intersection before reaching US 340). Park and Ride parking area is on the right.

Southern end of section at Harpers Ferry: From US 340, turn onto Shenandoah St (the "entrance" road for Harpers Ferry National Historical Park), at west end of bridge over Shenandoah River. Free parking in small lot (NAD83 N39° 19.298', W77° 44.590') marked "River Access" on corner of Shenandoah St and US 340. Overnight parking prohibited; lot usually fills early on weekends. From lot, take footpath on east side of road 0.3 mi into historic area of Harpers Ferry following an old canal that once served a thriving industrial complex on Virginius Island much of the way. Continue to end of Shenandoah St to reach *AT*. Parking also available for $10 at old train station (NAD83 N39° 19.479', W77° 43.906') in the old town, weekends only. For additional parking, at $10 per car, stay on US 340 and proceed to Harpers Ferry Visitor Center (NAD83 N39° 18.989', W77° 45.424').

Park and take tour bus back to historic area of Harpers Ferry. Continue to end of Shenandoah St to reach *AT*.

Overnight parking is available at the National Park Service Visitor Center. Pay admission fee at the main Visitor Center parking lot, then park on far side of lot, away from Visitor Center. Go to Visitor Center building (open 8 a.m. to 5 p.m.) and register for overnight parking. Parking is allowed in this lot for up to 14 days.

Maps
PATC Map 6 and USGS Harpers Ferry Quadrangle.

Shelters, Campsites, and Other Public Facilities
Harpers Ferry Hostel, part of the Hostel International Network, has 33 bunks in dorms and separate rooms for men, women, and family groups. It is open from 7:00 a.m. to 10:00 p.m., Apr 15-Dec 1. It does not provide meals, but offers full kitchen and laundry facilities, indoor toilets and showers, phone and Internet access, and other amenities. The per-night fee for beds is $18 for dorm rooms and $40 per night for private rooms. Camping in the large yard costs $6 per person per night. Use a credit card to make a reservation at 301-834-7652 or email HarpersFerry@hiusa.org.

SECTION HIGHLIGHTS

Israel Creek - A dirt "road" and pilings of a former bridge may be seen along Israel Creek, the deep ravine on the west near the US 340 overpass. These mark the route of the former Washington County Railroad, which later became the Hagerstown Branch of the Baltimore & Ohio Railroad.

Chesapeake & Ohio Canal - The 184.5 mile canal, which linked Washington and Cumberland, was completed in 1850. Operation ended in 1924, after the canal was severely damaged by a storm.

N-S

TRAIL DESCRIPTION

0.0 Northern end of section at Park and Ride parking **3.3**
lot, located on south side of Weverton Rd.
Southbound: Enter *AT* from center of Park and
Ride parking lot. Ahead parallel **Israel Creek,** on
right. Northbound: Reach Park and Ride parking
lot on south side of Weverton Rd.. To continue on
Trail, bear right and parallel Weverton Rd on trail
at foot of embankment.

0.2 Cross under US 340 overpass. **3.1**

0.4 Continue straight ahead, across grassy median **2.9**
triangle in middle of road. Southbound: Reach
NPS gate. Bear right and cross CSX (formerly
Baltimore & Ohio) Railroad tracks. Northbound:
Reach *AT* blaze and trail. For Sandy Hook Hostel,
see "Section Highlights."

0.5 Southbound: Cross causeway over abandoned **2.8**
Chesapeake & Ohio Canal. Turn right onto
towpath. Northbound: Turn left off towpath and
onto dirt road used by NPS ground maintenance
crews. Cross over canal, cross CSX (formerly
Baltimore & Ohio) Railroad tracks and bear left to
NPS gate.

2.0 Cross under Rte 340 Bridge, near **Sandy Hook**, and **1.3**
continue on towpath.

2.7 Pass canal lock. **0.6**

S-N

The canal is now a National Historical Park. Trail blazes will be found occasionally on posts along the canal's towpath.

Sandy Hook – The little town of Sandy Hook, on the other side of the tracks, was a "wild" town during the height of the canal and railroad transportation era.

The hostel is on Sandy Hook Rd, just outside the town of the same name and near the Maryland end of the US 340 bridge over the Potomac. A grocery store, motel, and restaurant all are in Sandy Hook near the Maryland end of the US 340 bridge over Potomac River. Reach all via Keep Tryst Rd (0.4/2.9 mi) or – at your own risk and using great caution – by way of an unmarked trail across canal and railroad track at bridge abutment (at mile 2.0 southbound and 1.3 northbound). The railroad officially prohibits use of the latter crossing, but using the authorized crossing means a long walk on a curving country road, often with little or no shoulder on which to avoid traffic.

Sandy Hook Store faces the unmarked trail, across Sandy Hook Rd, as you cross the tracks. To reach hostel, turn right and proceed uphill for 0.4 mi. To reach motel and restaurant, continue past the hostel on Sandy Hook Rd for 0.1 mile, take a left on Keep Tryst Rd and travel another 0.2 mi.

Goodloe Byron Memorial Footbridge – Congressman Goodloe E. Byron, 1928-78, was a great supporter of the *AT*. Along the footbridge, and at overlook near the bridge's south entrance, are superb view of the confluence of the Potomac and Shenandoah rivers. There is a bulletin board, and an adjacent post bears map of *AT* route through town. Look for new blazes on lampposts.

TRAIL DESCRIPTION

3.1   **Goodloe Byron Memorial Footbridge**.   **0.2**
Southbound: Pass under the first of two trestles, turn left, and ascend metal stairs of footbridge to cross river. Northbound: Turn right onto Chesapeake & Ohio Canal towpath. Trail blazes will be found occasionally on posts along towpath. Hikers wishing to reach the Grant Conway Maryland Heights Trail should follow the canal towpath west 0.4 mile. (See section on "*Side Trails*.")

3.3   Southern end of section, in Harpers Ferry, is at south   **0.0**
end of **Goodloe Byron Memorial Footbridge** over the river. Southbound: To continue on Trail, turn right and pass under trestle. Northbound: At end of Shenandoah St, turn right, pass under trestle, and follow walkway on left to footbridge. Cross Potomac River.

AT crosses the Potomac River   © Van Hill

View from Jefferson Rock   Darrell Midgette

HARPERS FERRY

GENERAL INFORMATION

Harpers Ferry is one of the outstanding historical and scenic attractions on the *AT*. The historic "lower town" area of Harpers Ferry, and much of the surrounding landscape became a National Historical Park in 1963. From north to south, the Trail passes near the scene of John Brown's raid, and then makes its way along the slope of a cliff, past the famous Jefferson Rock.

Two key *AT* offices are located in Harpers Ferry: (1) the headquarters of the Appalachian Trail Conservancy, and (2) the Appalachian Trail Park Office of the National Park Service.

HISTORY

Peter Stephens, a trader, settled in Harpers Ferry (then called "The Hole") in 1733 and established ferries across both rivers. Robert Harper purchased "squatter's rights" from Stephens and purchased the land, in 1747, from the legal holder, Lord Fairfax. The following spring, Fairfax engaged Peter Jefferson (father of Thomas) to survey the land. The survey party included 15-year-old George Washington, who later revisited this area several times before designating Harpers Ferry as the site for a national arsenal in 1796.

Beginning in the late 1700s, water transportation was improved with bypass canals around the rapids of the two rivers. The C&O Canal along the Potomac to Georgetown (Washington, D.C.) began operations from Harpers Ferry in the early 1830s, providing access to Tidewater markets. During the same time period in the early nineteenth century, Harpers Ferry became an important transportation and industrial center, attracting a produce center, hotels, saloons, and livery stables to service the town. The relatively flat route through the mountains along the river also attracted the B&O Railroad which soon gave the C&O Canal strong competition. The Railroad eventually became the dominant transportation provider. Here, in downtown Harpers Ferry, the Winchester and Potomac Railroad along the Shenandoah River connects with the main line. The C&O canal survived for almost a century, and was abandoned in the 1920s. Today, the towpath of the canal is "a natural" for a hiking trail. The towpath, across the Potomac from the town, leads downriver approximately 61 miles to Washington and upriver 124 to Cumberland.

An interesting historical and nature hike of 1.5 miles is found on Virginius Island. One of the National Park Service publications available at the Visitor Center describes the natural and historical features. Here was the site of an industrial village: a cotton textile mill with gas lighting, sawmill, flour mill, iron foundry, rolling mill, carriage factory, rifle factory and row houses. The rifle factory was built by James Hall, one of early developers of interchangeable parts for mass production. The entire industrial complex depended on water power, the source for industrial energy in the early 1800s. As you walk along the trails, you will be able to see many of the underground culverts which carried the head races and tail races for the water-powered mills Devastated by flood, fire, and war, the area now approximates the natural conditions when white explorers first arrived, except for a few ruins from the 1800s which have been excellently restored. The main man-made feature today is the railroad along the Shenandoah River, which divides the island in two. Be careful when crossing the tracks. This is the Winchester and Potomac Railroad, which was merged into the B&O Railroad company very soon after the B&O reached Harpers Ferry in the 1830s. Heavy freight trains still use this route today.

Harpers Ferry never recovered from John Brown's raid in 1859 and the following Civil War. (The Brown raid and the role of Harpers Ferry in the Civil War are more fully explained in the displays at the Visitor Center.) In addition to war, fire, and flood, epidemics of cholera and typhoid ravaged the town. The town would not have been likely to stay important as an industrial center anyway: Technological advancements in power no longer made it necessary to locate factories at the water's edge, where floods were a recurring threat.

Most of the historic section of the town lay in ruins when the Harpers Ferry National Monument (a designation of the National

Park Service) was provided for in a congressional enabling act of 1944. The first land was acquired in 1952, and the Federal parkland was renamed Harpers Ferry National Historical Park 1963. In addition to the downtown facilities and Virginius Island, land extending to Loudoun Heights across the Shenandoah, Bolivar Heights, and Elk Ridge to a point beyond the Stone Fort in Maryland, have been added. In the 1990s, the northern tip of Short Hill Mountain in Virginia was added to the Park, to protect the view down the Potomac River from Jefferson Rock in Harpers Ferry. Almost a thousand more acres were added between 1999 and 2004, mainly in West Virginia, in order to protect battleground areas that were a significant part of the siege of Harpers Ferry during the Civil War.

POINTS OF INTEREST

Buildings in downtown Harpers Ferry have been restored to the 1859-65 era. Currently, buildings and interior exhibits are open from 8 a.m. to 6 p.m. daily. A slide program and exhibits tell the history of Harpers Ferry and the story of John Brown's raid. (Restrooms are located in the building adjacent to the Harpers Ferry Historical Association bookstore.) The Master Armorer's House, down Shenandoah Street from the Visitor Center, contains an exhibit on gun making.

The fire engine house where Brown and his men made their last stand was originally located across Potomac Street on the site marked by a stone obelisk. The original building was removed from Harpers Ferry for several exhibits in different parts of the country. The current firehouse is slightly smaller than the original; many of the original bricks were taken for souvenirs during the periods when it was dismantled.

Store windows along Shenandoah Street display merchandise of a century ago, as well as tools and artifacts unearthed in the restoration and archaeological excavations. Foundations of the arsenal and a trench showing destroyed muskets are visible. The foundations of some of the rectangular armory buildings may be seen on the Potomac River side of the town in a slightly hidden area by the river next to the current railroad station.

The *AT* passes the house where Robert Harper lived during the last years of his life. Built between 1775 and 1781, it is the oldest surviving structure in town. It was restored by the Park Service and furnished with period pieces by the Women's Clubs of the county. The building is open daily.

The *AT* also passes Jefferson Rock, which is on a bluff overlooking the Shenandoah and the gap across to Loudoun Heights. The present Jefferson Rock is a flat stone supported by red sandstone pillars rising from a larger rock at the edge of the cliff.

Jefferson described the views in his "Notes on Virginia" in 1782:

"You stand on a very high point....On your right comes up the Shenandoah....On your left approaches the Potomac, in quest of a passage also. In the moment of their junction, they rush together against the mountain, render it asunder, and pass off to the sea.... For the mountain being cloven asunder, she presents to your eye, through the cleft, a small catch of smooth blue horizon, at an infinite distance of the plain country....This scene is worth a voyage across the Atlantic. Yet here, as in the neighborhood of the Natural Bridge, are people who have passed their lives within a half a dozen miles, and have never been to survey these monuments of a war between rivers and mountains..."

There are several excellent visitor centers with more information about the area.

The Appalachian Trail Visitor Center is located in the Appalachian Trail Conservancy headquarters. This is in the residential area of Harpers Ferry, at 799 Washington Street, at the junction with Storer College Place.

Contact information for the Appalachian Trail Conservancy/ Appalachian Trail Visitor Center:
P.O. Box 807
Harpers Ferry, WV 25425-0807
Phone: 304.535.6331
Fax: 304.535.2667
Website: http://www.appalachiantrail.org/home

Harpers Ferry National Historical Park

The main National Park Service Visitor Center for Harpers Ferry is on Cavalier Heights, just outside the built-up area of Harpers Ferry, at 171 Shoreline Drive, Harpers Ferry, WV 25425. To reach the Park Service Visitor Center from points east, take US 340 from Frederick, Maryland, heading westward in the direction of Charles Town West Virginia. Shortly after crossing the Potomac River and passing through a stoplight in Virginia, enter West Virginia. Continue on US 340 for a short section along the Rivers, first following the Potomac River and then the Shenandoah River. US 340 crosses the Shenandoah on the same bridge as the Appalachian Trail, and enters the town of Harpers Ferry. Beyond the Shenandoah River, continue up a hill on US 340 for one mile, ending at a crossroads and stoplight. This crossroads is the junction of Washington Street and Shoreline Drive with US 340. Turn Left onto Shoreline Drive, and follow the signs for Harpers Ferry National Historical Park.

This main Visitor Center for Harpers Ferry National Park has plenty of parking. There is an admission fee for the park – if coming by car, the charge is $10 for a three-day pass. The per-person charge is $5, also for a three-day pass. The $5 charge is for people coming on foot or by bicycle. From the Visitor Center, there is a shuttle bus that takes visitors to the historic Lower Town area of Harpers Ferry, where most of the museums and exhibits are located. The Visitor Center hours are 9:00 a.m. to 5:00 p.m., seven days a week, and the shuttle bus runs from 9:00 a.m. to 5:45 p.m. A hiking trail also connects the Visitor Center with the Lower Town. Parking in the Lower Town is extremely limited, so visitors are strongly encouraged to use the shuttle bus service and the large parking lot at the main Visitor Center. A smaller National Park Service parking lot is at the Harpers Ferry Train Station in the Lower Town. The Train Station Parking lot is in use by Commuters Monday through Friday, with limited spaces available on Saturday and Sunday, the days when MARC train service is not available. The National Park entrance charges apply for visitors using the Train Station parking lot, with free parking for MARC and Amtrak rail passengers.

Harpers Ferry National Historical Park contact information:
P.O. Box 65 Harpers Ferry, WV 25425
Visitor information: (304) 535-6029
Fax: (304) 535-6244
Website: www.nps.gov/hafe

The Harpers Ferry/Bolivar Community

The Jefferson County, West Virginia Convention and Visitors Bureau has a Tourist Information Center very close to U.S. Route 340 in the Harpers Ferry/Bolivar community. To reach the Tourist Information Center from points east of Harpers Ferry, follow the same directions for the main National Park Service Visitor Center up to the point where you get to the stoplight at the crossroads with West Washington Street and Shoreline Drive. Rather than turning in to the National Park Visitor Center, turn right onto West Washington Street. Look for the small, white colored "Tourist Information" building on the left. In less than half a block, turn left onto Washington Court. Immediately after entering Washington Court, park at one of the spaces next to the Tourist Information Center, which is in a temporary building next to a large Cedar model house for Lindal homes. The Tourist Information Center is at 37 Washington Court, Harpers Ferry, WV 25425

Contact information for the Jefferson County Convention and Visitors Bureau:
Phone: (304) 535-2627 or (304) 535-1813
Toll free: 1-866-HELLO-WV (1-866-435-5698)
Website: www.wveasterngateway.com

West Virginia Statewide tourist information:
Toll free: 1-800-CALL WVA (1-800-225-5982)
Website: http://www.wvtourism.com

References

Joseph Barry, *The Strange Story of Harpers Ferry* (The Shepherdstown Register, WV, 1958).   Republished by the Harpers Ferry Historical Association. Website: www.harpersferryhistory.org

E. L. Bowen, *Rambles in the Path of the Steam Horse* (Philadelphia: Wm. Brownell and Wm. White Smith, 1854).

Philip S. Forner, *Basic Writings of Thomas Jefferson* (New York: Wiley, 1944).

Paula Strain, *The Blue Hills of Maryland* (Vienna, Virginia: Potomac Appalachian Trail Club).

David T. Gilbert, *A Walker's Guide to Harpers Ferry* (Harpers Ferry, West Virginia: Harpers Ferry Historical Association).

Overview of *AT* Location in Northern Virginia and West Virginia

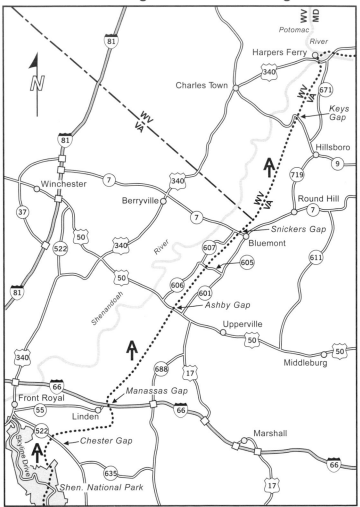

NORTHERN VIRGINIA AND WEST VIRGINIA

GENERAL INFORMATION
Distance: 57.5 Miles

This segment of the *AT* begins at the southern end of the Goodloe Byron Memorial Footbridge in Harpers Ferry. For about 14 miles after leaving Harpers Ferry it follows the ridge crest that forms the boundary between Virginia and West Virginia. It zigzags across the state line, with its total mileage in West Virginia (including Harpers Ferry) somewhat over 7 miles.

After a steep climb from the bridge over the Shenandoah River to the crest, the Trail follows the narrow crest of the Blue Ridge south past ruined stone breastworks of the Civil War period, through a section frequently burned over. This was the first section of Trail that the PATC constructed, in 1927-28. Some of this area is now included in the Harpers Ferry National Historical Park.

On each side of Snickers Gap, the *AT* skirts a long-established summer community. From Crescent Rock to Ashby Gap, land closings have forced the Trail off the main ridge and onto a route that crosses a succession of side ridges and hollows. Within this section, the *AT* passes Mt. Weather, a classified government installation operated by the Federal Emergency Management Agency.

For similar reasons, the Trail snakes along the slopes on each side of the Blue Ridge from Ashby Gap to Manassas Gap. The relocation of the Trail in these two sections represents one of the PATC's foremost successes in Trail protection.

South of Manassas Gap, the Trail climbs, east of Linden, over an abandoned, mountaintop farm with fine views and passes over the slopes of High Knob before descending to the west of Chester Gap. Then the Trail passes through the woods and fields of Harmony Hollow, on the western side of the Blue Ridge, to Shenandoah National Park.

From north to south, the Blue Ridge changes from a narrow ridge to a wider expanse of side ridges and outlying mountains. This is accompanied by an increase in the variety of growth that can be seen along the Trail.

The Trail in this chapter has been divided into the following sections:
1. Harpers Ferry to Keys Gap 6.3 mi
2. Keys Gap to Snickers Gap 13.5 mi
3. Snickers Gap to Ashby Gap 14.1 mi
4. Ashby Gap to Manassas Gap 11.8 mi
5. Manassas Gap to Chester Gap 8.2 mi
6. Chester Gap to Shenandoah National Park 3.6 mi

HISTORY ALONG THE TRAIL

The newly formed Potomac Appalachian Trail Club opened the Appalachian Trail south of Harpers Ferry in 1927, the first part of the Appalachian Trail to be established between the Hudson Valley and the Great Smokies. Within two years, a handful of members had made the Trail a reality as far as Rockfish Gap. Their work inspired the formation of other groups, which completed other links in the 2,000-mile footpath.

The PATC appointed its first Trail overseer in this region. Within two years of its opening, the original section of Trail was nearly lost because of fire, undergrowth and neglect. Walter R. Jex was assigned to maintain the *AT* from Harpers Ferry to Bluemont, a distance of 18 miles. Other PATC members soon took responsibility for other Trail sections, and the system of Trail overseers was born.

Early History

History in the conventional sense has happened only in bits and pieces along the Trail south of Harpers Ferry, while to the west in the Shenandoah Valley it has occurred on the grand scale. The natural barrier of the Blue Ridge has helped to channel settlement, commerce, and even war into the great flow of history up and down the valley. Along the Trail, however, we speak more of men crossing the ridge on missions of importance to the lands below.

Before the coming of the white man, this region was sparsely settled by tribes of the Powhatan Confederation to the east and by the Shawnees to the west. Other tribes, mentioned in the Maryland section of this Guide, used two great trails for war and migration. East of the ridge, in Loudoun and Fauquier counties, lay the Great War Road. To the west, in the Shenandoah Valley, was the major Indian trail that later became the chief route for white men as well; that trail is now known locally as the Valley Pike and more generally as US 11.

The first explorer to cross the Blue Ridge was a German, John Lederer, who made three successive trips to the Blue Ridge in March and May of 1669 and in August of 1670. On this last trip he discovered the northern pass into the Shenandoah Valley, probably Chester Gap, since he ascended the Rappahannock. The monument commemorating his discovery is located at Manassas Gap, however, just off the *AT* at Linden, Va. In 1707, the French explorer Louis Michelle led a party from Maryland into the Shenandoah Valley at Harpers Ferry and traveled as far south as Massanutten Mountain.

Settlement in the Blue Ridge began in the 1720s when German immigrants moved south from Pennsylvania, taking up land in the middle section of the Shenandoah Valley. The lower valley was not fully settled until after the French and Indian War, when Virginia planters moved in from the Tidewater.

The Appalachian Trail in northern Virginia and West Virginia lies within the original grant of Charles II to the Lords Fairfax, which conveyed all lands between the Potomac and Rappahannock rivers. Much was sold for settlement (and some taken by squatters), but in 1736 Thomas Lord Fairfax ordered a 120,000-acre tract surveyed, which he established as his Manor of Leeds. This included the entire Blue Ridge from Snickers Gap to Chester Gap and much of the Shenandoah Valley adjacent to it. When Fairfax settled in Virginia in 1748, he built his manor house, Greenway Court, near White Post. His surveyor that year was a 16-year-old lad named George Washington.

The Manor of Leeds was subsequently divided into lesser manors, all of which figured in speculation during the region's first land boom. A syndicate, consisting of John Marshall, James Marshall, and their brother-in-law Raleigh Colston, acquired the Manor in 1793. A clouded title prevented them from selling land, however, nearly bringing financial ruin until the courts cleared the title in 1806.

Blue Ridge Gaps

Five gaps in the Blue Ridge have always provided the essential contacts in northern Virginia between the Piedmont and the Shenandoah Valley. Known by various names in the past, they are now called Keys Gap, Snickers Gap, Ashby Gap, Manassas Gap, and Chester Gap.

Keys Gap, formerly Vestal's Gap, was served by a ferry on the Shenandoah as early as 1747, where at that time the region had its first iron industry. Washington used this route in 1754 during the campaign to Great Meadows and Fort Necessity, as did part of Braddock's army in 1755. (The name has variously been spelled Keys and Keyes; in February 1964, however, the Board of Geographic Names of the U.S. Geological Survey decided on Keys.)

Snickers Gap was named for Edward Snicker, who operated a ferry across the Shenandoah before 1764. It was originally known as Williams Gap, but has had its present name through most of its history. Snicker's name did not stick to the ferry, however, which became known as Castleman's. Washington used this route in his later years when he visited his cousin at Berryville and his brothers at Charles Town.

Ashby Gap was originally called the Upper Thoroughfare of the Blue Ridge and was served at the Shenandoah by Berry's Ferry. The main road to the valley, the Winchester Pike, passed through the gap, and it was along this route that Washington traveled on his first trip to the valley in 1748. Cornwallis's captured troops were marched through the gap to Winchester in 1781.

Ashby Gap received its present name from the Indian fighter, Colonel John Ashby, whose family settled near what is now Paris. The name also brings to mind his noted descendent General Turner Ashby, Confederate cavalry leader under General Stonewall Jackson.

Manassas Gap (Manassa's Gap, according to a probably apocryphal legend) was at one time known as Calmes Gap, after Marquis Calmes, a colonial figure whose name also appears on a bend of the Shenandoah River known as Calmes Neck.

Chester Gap once went by the name Happy Creek Gap.

Railroad Development

These gaps naturally attracted considerable interest during the railroad-building era, especially after the B&O preempted the Potomac water-level route at Harpers Ferry. Because of its low elevation, Manassas Gap was the most attractive, and by 1854 a railroad by that name ran from its junction with the Orange and Alexandria Railroad at Manassas through the gap to Strasburg in the Shenandoah Valley.

One other railroad scheme involved both Keys Gap and Snickers Gap. This is remembered by many area residents as the Washington & Old Dominion Railroad, which served Bluemont from 1900 to 1939. The railroad originated in the 1840s as the Alexandria, Loudoun & Hampshire Railroad, which was to reach Winchester by way of Vestal's (Keys) Gap. Financial troubles dogged the line, and it had only reached the Catoctin Ridge by the Civil War. After a change of name to Washington, Ohio & Western (WOW), a change in route to Snickers Gap, and receivership, the rails finally came to Snickersville in 1900. That same year the town adopted a more euphonious name, Bluemont.

Construction of the railroad to Bluemont may have influenced the building of many turn-of-the-century summer homes in the Bluemont area. This early development made it difficult to locate a route for the Appalachian Trail when it was later established.

Civil War Action

The Blue Ridge figured prominently in many Civil War actions. Jackson marched his troops through Ashby Gap on July 18, 1861, before the First Battle of Bull Run. They bivouacked at Paris before boarding the Manassas Gap Railroad to reach the battle just in time.

A year later, in September 1862, Confederate troops under Jackson's command climbed Loudoun Heights to bombard Harpers Ferry and forced its surrender with 11,000 Union troops just before the Battle of Antietam. Also on Loudoun Heights, the Confederate raider,

Colonel John S. Mosby, attempted to overrun a sleeping encampment of Maryland cavalry on January 10, 1864. He was discovered before he could spring the attack and was repulsed by half-dressed Union soldiers after a sharp fight that resulted in four deaths on each side.

To the south, Snickers Gap witnessed the retreat of General Jubal Early in July 1864, after his raid on Washington, D.C. In this gap in November 1864, Union troops laid an ambush for John Mobley, a former Mosby follower who led his own band to harass Union forces around Harpers Ferry. His death was largely due to information received after a $1,000 reward was put on his head.

The entire region from Snickers Gap to Manassas Gap and east to the Bull Run Mountains was under the influence of Colonel Mosby, the "gray ghost," and soon earned the name of "Mosby's Confederacy." Mosby's men lived in farmhouses throughout the region and gathered on command for their operations. Paris and Linden were frequent rendezvous sites.

South of Ashby Gap is Signal Knob, one of several promontories in the region used regularly for communications by both sides during the Civil War.

Scientific Activities

After the war, the most notable developments on the Blue Ridge occurred near Snickers Gap and brought science to the forefront. In October 1868, near Bears Den Rocks, Dr. Mahlon Loomis conducted one of the most significant but unrecognized experiments of the time, whereby he nearly discovered the existence of radio waves and operated the first radio antenna. He and a colleague on Catoctin Ridge, 18 miles away, simultaneously raised kites with copper gauze attached, on a copper wire, which was attached to a galvanometer. In a prearranged sequence, the two men attached one or the other galvanometer to ground wires and secured readings on the opposite instrument. Loomis thought of electricity as being like an ocean with a force that resembled waves of ripples; his purpose was to develop a form of aerial telegraph. This experiment took place 20 years before Hertz demonstrated the existence of radio waves.

In 1900 Professor Willis L. Moore, Chief of the U.S. Weather Bureau, proposed bringing together on the Blue Ridge a number of advanced weather research activities. Thus, in 1901, Mount Weather began operation with the eventual goal of investigating terrestrial magnetism, thermodynamics of the atmosphere, solar-physical and upper air phenomena, and model weather research. Work did not get underway uniformly on all projects, but early in 1907 the Mount Weather Station achieved the highest ascent of a kite in history (five miles). This ascent provided invaluable instrument recordings on the upper atmosphere. After 1907, however, the Mount Weather project languished, and occasional proposals were offered to revive the facility for various purposes. One such was to make it a summer White House during the Coolidge administration. In recent years, Mount Weather has been developed as a classified government installation, and is closed to public entry.

West of the Appalachian Trail in Chester Gap lies another government installation with an interesting past. The U.S. Army originally acquired it in 1911 as a remount station to provide a supply of horses and mules. Later it served as a prisoner-of-war camp, and was also used for training K-9 dogs. Its usefulness to the Army diminished after the war, and in 1948 the property was transferred to the U.S. Department of Agriculture, which used it as a beef cattle research station and conference center. These operations were discontinued in the early 1970s, and the facility and land were transferred to the National Zoological Park (for a Research and Conservation Center) and to Virginia Polytechnic Institute (for a 4-H center).

Trail Route Status

Although the *AT* route in northern Virginia and West Virginia was one of the earliest parts of the Trail, this does not mean that the route is well established. From the start, relatively little was on public property. Some private property owners have, over the years, been increasingly reluctant to have the Trail cross their property. Where a key piece of property is involved, long sections of Trail have been effectively blocked.

In the last few years, the National Park Service land acquisition program has protected a permanent, woodland route for nearly the entire northern Virginia and West Virginia stretch. This protection effort was aided by key purchases by the PATC in the early stages, and by the cooperation of the state of Virginia.

West Virginia History

In 1863 West Virginia became a state, and Jefferson County, Virginia, became a part of the new state. Along the state line the Appalachian Trail meanders back and forth using the best geographical features of the top of the Blue Ridge.

SELECTED REFERENCES

Davis, Julia, *The Shenandoah* (New York: Rinehart, 1945).

Harwood, Herbert H. Jr., *Rails to the Blue Ridge* (Falls Church, Va.: Pioneer American Society, 1969).

Leighton, Marion, "Mosby's Confederacy," *PATC Bulletin*, January 1939.

Loudoun County Civil War Centennial Commission, *Loudoun County and the Civil War: A History and Guide* (Leesburg, Va., 1961).

Schairer, Frank, "Early Days of the Appalachian Trail," *PATC Bulletin*, July-September 1969.

Solyom, Herbert L., "Mount Weather," *PATC Bulletin*, January 1941.

Strain, Paula, "Kite String Antenna," *PATC Bulletin*, December 1968.

Wayland, John W., *Twenty-five Chapters on the Shenandoah Valley* (Strasburg, Va.: Shenandoah Publishing House, 1957).

Wellman, Manley Wade, *Harpers Ferry, Prize of War*, (Charlotte, NC: McNally, 1960).

View from Bears Den Rocks   Aaron Watkins

AT Elevation Profile -- Virginia Section 1

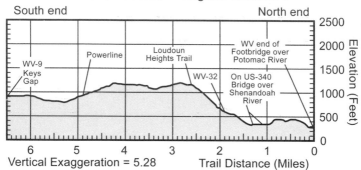

View from Weverton Cliffs   Bill Cooke

Section 1
HARPERS FERRY TO KEYS GAP
Distance: 6.3 Miles

This is a relatively easy section, especially for northbound hikers, who face a net descent of about 600 feet. The footing is good except for a rough 1.3 mi segment. There is an excellent viewpoint at Jefferson Rock (at 0.2/6.0 mi). Several rock redoubts, built as Civil War defenses for Harpers Ferry, may be seen beside the Trail between 2.3/3.9 mi and 2.6/3.7 mi. For additional points of interest, see chapter for Harpers Ferry.

Road Access
Northern end of section at Harpers Ferry: From US 340, turn onto Shenandoah St (the "entrance" road for Harpers Ferry National Historical Park) at west end of bridge over Shenandoah River. Parking in small lot on corner of Shenandoah St and US 340 (NAD83 N39° 19.298', W77° 44.590'), identified by sign for "River Access." Overnight parking prohibited. (This lot usually fill early on weekends.) From lot, take footpath on east side of road 0.3 mi into historic area of Harpers Ferry. Continue to end of Shenandoah St to reach *AT*. For additional parking, at $10 per car, stay on US 340 and proceed to Harpers Ferry NPS Visitor Center (NAD83 N39° 18.989', W77° 45.424'). Park and take free shuttle bus to historic area of Harpers Ferry. Continue to end of Shenandoah St to reach *AT*. Additional parking, for $10, at train station in old town, *weekends only*.

Overnight parking is available at the National Park Service Visitor Center. Pay admission fee at the main Visitor Center parking lot, then park on far side of lot, away from Visitor Center. Go to Visitor Center building (open 8 a.m. to 5 p.m.) and register for overnight parking. Parking is allowed in this lot for up to 14 days.

Southern end of section at Keys Gap: This is on WVa 9. The *AT* crosses the highway a few yards from the state line. A parking area for about 12 cars lies beside the Trail, on the northern side of the highway (NAD83 N39° 15.668', W77° 45.729'). Hillsboro, VA is 6 miles east; Charles Town, WV is 7.4 miles west.

Maps
PATC Map 7 and USGS Harpers Ferry and Charles Town Quadrangles.

Shelters, Campsites, and Other Public Facilities
Camping and fires are prohibited in the Park. Harpers Ferry has a hotel, post office, and various stores and services. Detailed information can be obtained at ATC headquarters, on corner of Washington and Jackson streets. Camping also is prohibited between Keys Gap (6.3/0.0) and the high tension powerline (4.8/1.5 mi) to the north (approximately 1.5 mi).

Supplies
Stores with food and *water* lie 0.3 mi either side of *AT* at Keys Gap. Eastern store has pay phone and restrooms.

SECTION HIGHLIGHTS

Harpers Ferry National Historical Park – The park encompasses 2,500 acres of land in three states. The Park Visitor Center can be found on the east side of Shenandoah St., just south of High St.

Shenandoah St. – In the first block of Shenandoah St., on the east, is a replica of fire engine house in which John Brown made his stand. Old Federal arsenal foundations are adjacent.

Robert Harper's House – Built from 1775-1781, it is the town's oldest dwelling.

N-S	TRAIL DESCRIPTION	

0.0   Northern end of section begins in Harpers Ferry at   **6.3**
bulletin board at end of brick walkway in **Harpers
Ferry National Historical Park**. Overlook on
east has superb view of Potomac and Shenandoah
confluence. Southbound: An adjacent post bears
map of *AT* route through town. Look for blazes
painted on old lampposts. Turn right west and
walk under trestle. Reach **Shenandoah St**, and pass
straight across to Potomac St. In 1/2 block turn
left onto open courtyard. Northbound: Turn west
at bulletin board at beginning of brick walkway. To
continue on Trail, follow brick walkway to Goodloe
Byron Memorial Footbridge.

0.1   Southbound: Pass through courtyard, cross straight   **6.2**
over **High St** and ascend old stone steps. Ahead, pass
"Armory Workers' Apartments" on west and continue
straight up road, passing **Robert Harper's House** on
west corner and St. Peter's Roman Catholic Church
(1833) on east. Northbound: Pass **Jefferson Rocks**
on right and pass old church ruins on left and then
Catholic Church on right. Look for blazes on old
lampposts. Continue steeply down old stone steps,
cross High St and enter open courtyard. Turn right
at **Potomac St.** Cross straight over **Shenandoah St**
and walk under trestle.

SECTION HIGHLIGHTS

Jefferson Rock – This large, flat rock overlooks the confluence of the Potomac and Shenandoah rivers. The view was said by Thomas Jefferson to be "worth a voyage across the Atlantic."

ATC Headquarters and Visitor Center – Reached by a side trail at 0.7/5.6 mi or via High Street route from northern end of section (see below). Headquarters is located near intersection of Jackson and Washington. ATC is on the east corner. A post office is two blocks farther. To reach ATC headquarters from the intersection of High St and Shenandoah St, go south on High St (becomes Washington St) about 0.5 mi to its intersection with Jackson St. by a side trail at 0.7/5.6 mi or via High Street route from northern end of section (see below).

Storer College – Began in 1865 as a one-room school for former slaves. In 1881, Frederick Douglass gave his famous speech on abolitionist John Brown here. In 1938, it had grown to become a full-fledged small college. In 1954 the school desegregation decision meant the end of federal and state funding and the school closed in 1955. It is still used as a training facility.

N-S

TRAIL DESCRIPTION

0.2 Southbound: Go straight up steps, leaving road where road bears to west, and pass ruins of St. John's Episcopal Church (1852) on west. Seventy yards ahead, go west at fork by "Harper Cemetery" sign. Path on east side of Trail leads a few yards to excellent view from **Jefferson Rock**. Northbound: Pass ruins of St. John's Episcopal Church (1852) on west, descend steps, go straight onto paved road, and pass St. Peter's Roman Catholic Church (1833) on east. Where road bears to west, go straight down stone steps, passing **Robert Harper's House** and "Armory Workers' Apartments," both on west.   **6.1**

0.3 Path on west side of Trail leads a few yd to Harpers Cemetery. Southbound: Go straight at cross-paths. Ahead, Trail undulates along cliff. *Watch for poison ivy.* Northbound: Go straight at cross paths. Descend, sometimes steeply. Ahead, path on east leads a few yd to excellent view from **Jefferson Rock**.   **6.0**

0.4 Path on west leads to **Lockwood House**. Southbound: Go straight. Stay on cliff and ignore intersecting paths ahead. Northbound: Go east at fork.   **5.9**

0.7 Blue-blazed trail leads 0.2 mi west to **ATC Headquarters and Visitor Center**. Southbound: Go straight on Trail, veering east. Ahead, go west at fork. Northbound: Go straight on Trail, veering to east. Trail undulates ahead. Stay on cliff and ignore intersecting paths.   **5.6**

S-N

ATC Headquarters and Visitor Center

Appalachian Trail Conservancy

N-S	TRAIL DESCRIPTION	
1.0	Southbound: Descend cliff to junction of US 340 and Shenandoah St. Follow pedestrian walk across bridge over Shenandoah River. Northbound: Cross to east side of US 340 at junction of US 340 and Shenandoah St (the Park "entrance" road) in Harpers Ferry. Ascend cliff very steeply. (Watch for new lampposts with blazes.)	**5.3**
1.3	US 340 crossing. Note splendid winter view from cliff just south of crossing. Southbound: End of bridge. Turn east and descend steps. Follow walkway under US 340. Ascend steps up bank. Cross level area and enter woods. Northbound: Leave woods, cross level area. Descend steps down bank. Follow walkway under US 340, then ascend steps and turn west.	**5.0**
1.4	Cross ravine filled with hemlocks.	**4.9**
1.6	Cross ravine. Southbound: Ascend through beautiful, profuse growth of periwinkle.	**4.7**
1.7	Cross W Va 32, passing under powerline to south of highway. Southbound: Re-enter woods. Northbound: Descend on path through beautiful, profuse growth of periwinkle.	**4.6**
1.8	Southbound: Turn east. Trail parallels old gullied road. Northbound: Turn east, away from road.	**4.5**
1.9	Trail crosses gullied road. Southbound: Ahead, ascend very steeply at times, with occasional switchbacks. Northbound: Descend less steeply. Trail relocation work is planned in this area.	**4.4**

S-N

SECTION HIGHLIGHTS

Loudoun Heights Trail – Side blue blaze trail joins *AT* on east at 2.4/3.9. This is an "in and out" trail to Split Rock. See section on "*Side Trails*."

Civil War rock redoubts – When Lee invaded Maryland in 1862, he detailed Jackson to capture Harpers Ferry, which fell after a short siege, Sept. 13-15. Brigadier General John G. Walker's division bombarded the town from these heights. The redoubts were infantry defenses built and abandoned by the Federals.

Blue Ridge Center for Environmental Stewardship – This 894-acre facility offers woods and streams, a working farm, wildflower meadows, historic farmsteads, wildlife, farm animals, and more. The facility uses educational programs and land use practices to show the connections between people and the natural world, and to demonstrate ecological and economic sustainability. A variety of visitor and volunteer activities are available. The Center is open seven days a week, from dawn to dusk. Individuals, families and groups should call ahead, tel. 540-668-7640, for overnight camping.

	TRAIL DESCRIPTION	

2.1 Junction of *AT* and orange-blazed trail that leads straight ahead to Loudoun Heights Trail (see section on *"Side Trails"*). Southbound: Turn west at junction. Northbound: Turn west and descend very steeply at times, with occasional switchbacks. Trail relocation is planned in this area.   **4.2**

2.2 Turn west onto old road.   **4.1**

2.4 Ridge crest. Blue-blazed **Loudoun Heights Trail** joins *AT* from east (see section on *"Side Trails"*). Southbound: Turn west at junction. Ahead, leave Harpers Ferry National Historical Park and pass **Civil War rock redoubts**. Northbound: Enter **Harpers Ferry National Historical Park**. *Camping and fires are prohibited.* Then turn west and descend.   **3.9**

3.1 Southbound: Ascend steeply. Begin watching for poison ivy, which is predominant along Trail for remainder of this section. Northbound: Ascend.   **3.2**

3.4 Southbound: Level, with rocky footing ahead. Northbound: Footing becomes good again. Descend steeply.   **2.9**

4.4 Possible campsite on east.   **1.9**

4.8 Cross high-tension powerline clearing. Sign pointing to east indicates side trail that follows powerline access road and leads down mountain to **Blue Ridge Center for Environmental Stewardship**. Go straight at crossroad in center of corridor. View of Short Hill Mtn. to east, but western view is almost entirely blocked by summer growth. Southbound: Footing is good again. *No camping allowed from the powerline south to Keys Gap.* Northbound: Rocky footing ahead.   **1.5**

Loudon Heights view of Harpers Ferry John McDowell

N-S	TRAIL DESCRIPTION	

5.0 Southbound: Ascend slightly, then level. Rocky footing in places ahead. Continue to ascend and descend. Northbound: Ascend. Good footing. **1.3**

6.0 Old road intersects on west. Continue straight. **0.3**

6.3 Southern end of section at W Va 9 near Keys Gap. North of W Va 9 there is a bulletin board with *AT* information and a parking lot on west side of the Trail. Southbound: To continue on Trail, cross W Va 9. Northbound: Pass bulletin board and parking lot, located west of Trail. *No camping allowed between Keys Gap and the high tension powerline to the north (approximately 1.5 mi).* **0.0**

AT Elevation Profile -- Virginia Section 2

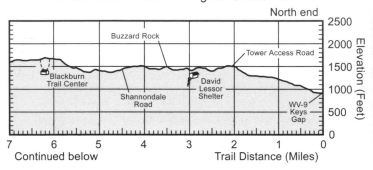

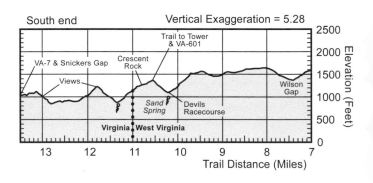

SECTION 2
KEYS GAP TO SNICKERS GAP
Distance: 13.5 Miles

This section, mostly along the ridge crest, offers an interesting hike with considerable variety. The length, numerous undulations, and occasional rocky footing make it one of the most rugged sections in this book. The southern three miles of this section begins a portion of the *AT* that has become known as the "Rollercoaster." This section is a moderately difficult day hike.

Points of interest include views from Buzzard Rocks (at 3.6/9.9 mi), from an outcrop (at 6.1/7.4 mi), from Crescent Rock (at 10.9/2.6 mi), which also has unusual rock formations, and from two outcrops (at 11.8/1.7 mi and 12.9/0.6 mi). Other points of geological interest are The Lookout (at 6.8/6.7 mi) and Devils Racecourse (at 10.3/3.2 mi). The misnamed Laurel Swamp (at 5.2/8.3 mi) has a beautiful growth of periwinkle and a former house site.

Road Access

Northern end of section at Keys Gap: Keys Gap is on Va 9. The *AT* crosses the highway on the West Virginia side of the state line. A parking area for about 12 cars lies beside the Trail, on the northern side of the highway (NAD83 N39° 15.668', W77° 45.729'). Hillsboro, Va., is 6 miles east; Charles Town, W. Va., is 7.4 miles west.

Southern end of section at Snickers Gap: Snickers Gap is on Va 7. The *AT* crosses Va 7 slightly west of the gap. Numerous cars can park on the southwest corner of Va 7 and Va 601 (NAD83 N39° 06.937', W77° 50.803'). Several cars can park where the *AT* leaves Va 679 (NAD83 N39° 06.986', W77° 51.151'). From Snickers Gap, Bluemont is 1.8 miles east.

Access to Blackburn Trail Center: From Va 7 or Va 9, take Woodgrove Rd. Turn onto *AT* Rd and follow it almost to the top of the ridge, avoiding all private driveways. Access to *AT* is by two side trails from Blackburn Trail Center (NAD83 N39° 11.239', W77° 47.860').

Maps

PATC Map 7 and USGS Charles Town, Round Hill, and Bluemont Quadrangles.

Shelters, Campsites, and Other Public Facilities

David Lesser Shelter (115 yd by side trail, at 3.0/10.5 mi) has a deck with bench and accommodates 6 persons under the roof. Facilities include covered picnic table, fireplace, and privy. A tenting area is located just below the shelter on the side trail to the spring. *Spring* is a quarter mile down hill.

Blackburn Trail Center Campground (0.1 mi by side trail, at 6.2/7.3 mi), maintained by the PATC, has tent sites and a privy. Use is free on a first-come, first-served basis. *Water* is available from an outside spigot by driveway entrance at the Blackburn Trail Center (0.2 mi by side trail at 6.4/7.1 mi), as is a Hiker Hostel that sleeps 8 (see highlights for more information).

Supplies

Stores with food and water lie 0.3 mi either side of *AT* at Keys Gap. Eastern store has pay phone and restrooms. Pine Grove Restaurant lies 0.9 mi north of *AT* on Va 679; closed Sunday afternoons and Mondays. Another 0.1 mi farther is a grocery store.

Water and a telephone are available at Blackburn Trail Center (0.2 by side trail at 6.4/7.1) (see highlights). Water is also available from *Sand Spring* (70 yd on side trail, at 10.3/3.2 mi).

There is a post office in Bluemont, which has a General Delivery mail-drop that can be used by hikers.

Blackburn Trail Center

SECTION HIGHLIGHTS

David Lesser Shelter – Reached by following side trail at 3.0/10.5 mi for 115 yd, has a deck with bench and accommodates 6 persons under the roof. Facilities include covered picnic table, swing, fireplace, and privy. Tenting area is located just below the shelter on trail to spring. *Spring* is quarter mile down steep hill.

Buzzard Rocks – Blue-blazed trail forks. The right branch leads to scree with no view, while left branch leads to Buzzard Rocks. Limited summer view of Shenandoah River and Shannondale Lake. *Watch for poison ivy.*

PATC shelter crew at work   Henry Horn

N-S

| | TRAIL DESCRIPTION | |

0.0 Northern end of section at W Va 9 in Keys Gap. **13.5**
Southbound: *AT* angles westward away from
highway, passing through field. *Watch for poison ivy.*

0.1 Cross polluted stream flowing from pond a short **13.4**
distance to west. Several paths in open woods make
Trail hard to follow. *Watch for blazes.*

1.1 Primitive campsite. **12.4**

1.6 Southbound: Go west at fork and ascend; 50 yd **11.9**
farther, cross old road. Northbound: Cross old road
and descend; in 50 yd faint old road joins from east.

2.0 Cross old road at south end of area with good winter **11.5**
views to east.

2.1 Reach north end of area with good winter view to **11.4**
east.

3.0 Blue-blazed trail leads east 115 yd to **David Lesser** **10.5**
Shelter. (*Spring* and overflow campsite 0.2 mi
farther downhill with room for 8-10 tent sites.)
Forest road (north) transitions to steep rocky path
(south).

3.6 Blue-blazed trail near top of rock outcrop leads **9.9**
west 0.1 mi to **Buzzard Rocks**. Southbound: *AT*
descends steeply over boulders just beyond turnoff.

3.7 Reach north end of rocky, sometimes narrow finger **9.8**
of trail 0.1 mi long.

4.1 Clearing with primitive campsite on low ground **9.4**
east of *AT*.

S-N

Old Shannondale Rd – Once connected Hillsboro to Shannondale Springs, a famous 19th-century resort that was patronized by Presidents.

"Laurel Swamp" – Beautiful, profuse growth of periwinkle covers former house site on west side of Trail. Rock walls outline yard, and slight chimney ruins are visible. Garden terraces rise above site.

Blackburn Trail Center – This PATC facility (540-338-9028) is staffed by PATC caretakers. On clear days, from the porch you may be able to glimpse the Washington Monument and National Cathedral in the distance, to the east. The Center has a bunkhouse that sleeps 8, with a wood-burning stove and a picnic pavilion. The picnic pavilion was built in 2002 with ALDHA donations in memory of Edward B. Garvey. Six tent sites and a tent platform are nearby, and a camping area with privy is 0.1 mi north of the main building on the blue-blazed trail. *Water* is available year-round from an outside spigot. A pay phone and log book are located on the porch, and a solar-heated shower is on the lower lawn. There is no charge for hikers staying overnight, but donations are always appreciated. PATC work and hiking groups are often here.

N-S	TRAIL DESCRIPTION	

4.5	Southbound: Go straight onto **Old Shannondale Rd** (now just a path which intersects from west), then fork west off road just ahead. Northbound: Turn west onto what remains of road, then bear east just ahead, as old road (now just a path) cuts west.	**8.9**
5.2	Cross wet area on boardwalk.	**8.3**
5.3	A few yd west are remains of walled-in *Laurel Spring*, which is often dry.	**8.1**
6.1	Path to quartzite outcrop on west offers good view.	**7.4**
6.2	Blue-blazed trail to east descends very steeply to campground (left fork in 0.1 mi) and to **Blackburn Trail Center** (0.2 mi). Southbounders may take a longer but somewhat gentler route to Center by continuing on Trail to second turnoff, 0.2 mi ahead.	**7.3**
6.4	Blue-blazed trail to east descends steeply to **Blackburn Trail Center** in 0.2 mi.	**7.1**
6.8	The Lookout, an unusual pile of boulders on east side of Trail, once offered a fine eastward view, hence the name. Trees have now completely blocked view. 50 yd south of pile, a low stone wall along west edge of trail marks point where a mountain road reached ridge and turned south along current route of *AT*.	**6.7**
7.6	Cross old sunken roadbed and ascend.	**5.9**
8.1	Ridge narrows and Trail levels along crest. A short scramble up boulders provides overlook to west.	**4.8**
8.8	Rocky knoll on west. Southbound: Ascend very steeply to reach this point. Northbound: Descend very steeply after this point.	**4.6**

S-N

Devils Racecourse – Trail crosses this boulder field at 10.3/3.1 mi. There is a small stream running beneath it. This feature is similar to its namesake in MD Section 1.

Ridge-to-River Trail – This is a 2.5-mile trail that drops down the west side of the Blue Ridge, ending at the Shenandoah River. PLEASE NOTE: This trail crosses private lands by permission. Please respect the owners' privacy and stay on the trail. There is no access from the west side of the mountain. For more information, see description in *"Side Trails"* section of this guide.

Crescent Rock – From here, the distinctive sloping terminus of Massanutten Mountain can be seen in the distance. A path leads west along cliff about 100 feet to point where cliff can be descended. By walking back, along base of cliff to foot of Crescent Rock, one can see the geological fold that forms a crescent in the rock. The core of the fold has been broken out by the action of ice in the crevices, forming a six-foot deep, arch-shaped indentation in the cliff. Pulpit Rock, or the "pinnacle," stands about 150 feet west of Crescent Rock. It is a column of rock that is separated from the cliff by a gap of about 10 feet. *(The danger of snakes makes it inadvisable to descend the cliff during warm weather.)*.

N-S	TRAIL DESCRIPTION	

9.2 Relatively level compared to Trail south of this point. Winter views to east from rocky crest. **4.3**

9.6 Ridgeline with rocky footing. Reach north end of Roller Coaster. **3.9**

10.2 Angle left across broad powerline clearing. Southbound: Cross under powerline and re-enter woods on old road. On left, paralleling road, is **Devils Racecourse**. Northbound: Turn west along powerline, then shortly leave it to ascend narrow, rocky trail. **3.3**

10.3 Old roadbed leading west reaches seasonal *Sand Spring* in 70 yd (on right), a year-round *spring* 20 yd farther on left, and blue-blazed **Ridge-to-River Trail**. Continue straight. Southbound: Turn east off road, across **Devil's Racecourse**, and ascend steeply. Northbound: Leave Devils Racecourse and turn east onto old road and ascend. **3.2**

10.7 Old road from transmission tower joins from east. Cross high saddle of Raven Rocks and begin descent. **2.8**

10.9 Trail twists to **Crescent Rock**, with excellent view west to Shenandoah River and Valley. **2.6**

11.0 Pass marker for Virginia/West Virginia border, which gives distance from Harpers Ferry as 17.4 mi **2.5**

11.2 Steep, 500-foot elevation change (ascending to north/descending to south), *slippery at all times*. **2.3**

Crescent Rock   Ling Nero

N-S	TRAIL DESCRIPTION	

11.3 Descend into saddle with rocky, sometimes dry streambed. Norway maples in this area. Blue-blazed trail to west leads to two *springs*. One spring is poor, the other has year-round water. Southbound: Go straight, then west at fork, cross rocky creek bed and ascend. Northbound: Bear west and cross rocky creek bed, then bear east at fork and ascend. **2.2**

11.8 At a high point, Trail bows west to good view of Shenandoah Valley from quartzite outcrop. Southbound: Descend steeply through black tupelo (blackgum), laurel, azaleas, and pine. Then, as descent gets easier, *watch for poison ivy*. Northbound: *Watch for poison ivy* as you begin ascent to this point. Climb begins gradually but becomes steep. After this viewpoint, Trail descends again. **1.7**

12.7 Cross stream in Pigeon Hollow. Southbound: After steep descent on log steps to this stream, ascend, steeply at times, by long switchbacks through rocks. Northbound: Ascend steeply on log steps. **0.8**

12.9 Fine view of southern Shenandoah Valley from rock outcrop at west edge of Trail. Northbound: Descend, steeply at times, by long switchbacks through rocks. Southbound: Continue ascent. **0.6**

13.5 Southern end of section at Va 7, slightly west of Snickers Gap. Post with *AT* sign in Va 7 median strip. (Bluemont is 1.8 mi east.) Southbound: To continue on Trail, cross Va 7 and turn left (uphill) on shoulder of road to *AT* blaze on right. Northbound: To continue on Trail, cross parking lot at Va 679, find Trailhead near bulletin board, and ascend. **0.0**

AT Elevation Profile -- Virginia Section 3

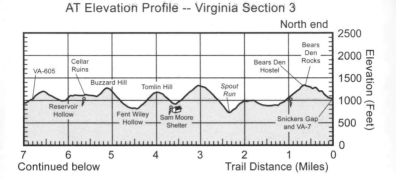

North end

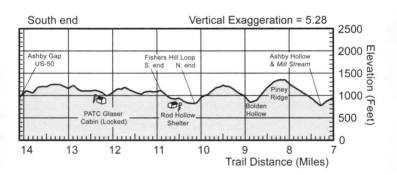

South end   Vertical Exaggeration = 5.28

SECTION 3
SNICKERS GAP TO ASHBY GAP
Distance: 14.1 Miles

Land closings have forced the *AT* off the main ridge in this section, but the Trail now follows a stable route on a protected corridor to the west. Consequently, the Trail seesaws in and out of a succession of hollows and over numerous side ridges, making this probably the most difficult section in this book, and is often referred to as "The Roller Coaster." (Poison ivy may be a problem in some areas.) Nevertheless, the route may be seen as an interesting contrast to the ridge-walking that dominates most of the *AT* route in Maryland and northern Virginia. There are excellent views from Bears Den Rocks (at 0.6/13.5 mi), Lookout Point (at 3.1/11.0 mi) and Buzzard Hill (at 5.0/9.1 mi). The dark and cool Fent Wiley Hollow (at 4.3/9.5 mi) has a great variety of mature timber. The Trail also passes a former cabin site (at 5.6/8.5 mi).

Road Access
Northern end of section at Snickers Gap: Snickers Gap is on Va 7. The *AT* crosses Va 7, 0.25 mi west of the gap. Numerous cars can park in the parking lot used by carpool participants, located on the southwest corner of Va 7 and Va 601 (NAD83 N39° 06.937', W77° 50.803'). There is a blue-blazed trail from the southwest side of the parking lot to the *AT*. Limited parking on northeast corner of Va 7 and Va 679 (NAD83 N39° 06.986', W77° 51.151'). From Snickers Gap, Bluemont is 1.8 miles east, and Washington, D.C., is about 52 miles east.

Southern end of section at Ashby Gap: This is on US 50. The *AT* crosses US 50, 0.25 mi west of the gap. PATC has a parking lot on the west side of Va 601, about 0.2 mile north of US 50 (NAD83 N39° 01.007', W77° 57.733'). A blue-blazed access trail at the back of the lot descends to the *AT* in 85 yd (at 13.9/0.2 mi). Paris is 1.0 mile east, and Washington, D.C., is 56 miles east.

Alternate access at Va 605 (Morgans Mill Rd.): Take Va 601 south from Snickers Gap, or north from Ashby Gap, and turn onto Va 605, a drivable dirt road, at Mt. Weather. There is room for a couple of cars to park on the powerline right-of-way, at the *AT* crossing (NAD83 N39° 04.327', W77° 54.716'), about 1.4 miles west of Va 601.

Maps
PATC Map 8 and USGS Bluemont and Paris Quadrangles.

Shelters, Campsites, and Other Public Facilities
Sam Moore Shelter (0.1 mi by side trail, at 3.6/10.5 mi) accommodates six persons. It stands next to *Sawmill Spring* and has a privy, fireplace, and sheltered picnic table. There are also two primitive tent sites.

Rod Hollow Shelter (0.1 mi by side trail, at 10.5/3.6 mi) accommodates seven persons. It has a *spring*, privy, and sheltered picnic table and hearth, as well as four tent sites.

Bears Den Hostel (0.2 mi by side trail, at 0.6/13.5 mi). See "Section Highlights."

Pine Grove Restaurant lies 0.9 mi north of Va 7 on Va 679. Closed Sunday afternoons and Mondays. Horseshoe Curve Restaurant is 0.3 mi north of Va 7 on Va 679. Open Tues-Sat, noon-10 p.m.; Sun noon-6 p.m.

Supplies
The hostel and restaurants (see above and "Section Highlights") have telephones. The Village Market grocery store at Snickers Gap lies 1.0 mile north of Va 7 on Va 679. *Water* is available at the Bears Den Hostel (see "Section Highlights"), and from *springs* at 0.9/13.2 mi, at 3.6/10.5 mi (intermittent), at 5.6/8.5 mi, and at Rod Hollow Shelter at 10.5/3.6 mi.

Bears Den Lodge and Hostel

SECTION HIGHLIGHTS

Bears Den Hostel – Is owned by ATC and operated by PATC. Phone 540-554-8708. Email: info@bearsdencenter.org. Website: www.bearsdencenter.org.

Bears Den is situated on a beautiful 66 acre property and features five primitive campsites, a large group site, and over two miles of trails for visitors of all skill levels. The lodge is a historic stone mansion featuring a great hall with fireplace, dining room, lodge store, and a fully equipped kitchen. Twin bunk rooms on the main floor, each with its own bathroom accommodate up to 20 people. The private room has one queen bed, two double bunks, and a bathroom. Bears Den Hostel has 10 bunks, a full bathroom, laundry facilities, and TV/internet access. Bed and bath linens are provided. The store sells maps and food, such as snacks, sodas, frozen pizza, and ice cream. All guests are welcome to enjoy a self-serve pancake breakfast.

On-site parking is available for vehicles; $3 daily. Hours, 7 days a week: Gate: 8:00 a.m.-9:00 p.m. Lodge: 5:00 p.m.-9:00 p.m. Hostel: 24 hours with access code. Rates: Hike/Bike (per person, first come, first served) $30: Hiker Special (bunk, laundry, pizza, ice cream, and soda) $17-Bunk: $12-lawn camp. Drive-in (per person, reservations required) $60-private room (2 people), $15 each additional: $23-Bunk: $9-campsite.

Sam Moore Shelter – Is reached in 0.1 mi by side trail and accommodates six persons. It has a privy, fireplace, sheltered picnic table, and two tent sites. *Sawmill Spring* is nearby. It is named in honor of a long-time dedicated PATC member.

N-S		
	TRAIL DESCRIPTION	

0.0	Section begins at median strip on Va 7, 0.25 mi west of Snickers Gap, at junction of Va 679. Southbound: Go east on south shoulder of Va 7 and turn south onto graveled driveway that narrows to a path almost immediately, ascending through dogwood, yellow poplar, oak, laurel, and sassafras. Northbound: On reaching Va 7 turn left and walk downhill on south shoulder for short distance. Turn right and cross Va 7 onto Va 679. Enter parking lot and find trail behind bulletin board and ascend.	**14.1**
0.2	Blue-blazed trail to parking lot enters *AT* from east.	**13.9**
0.6	Bears Den Rock to west has outstanding view of Shenandoah Valley. Loop path to east leads 0.2 mi to **Bears Den Lodge and Hostel** (*tap water* available).	**13.5**
1.2	Cross creek on footbridge.	**12.9**
2.4	Cross Spout Run in deep, narrow ravine.	**11.7**
3.0	Peak of ridge.	**11.1**
3.1	Lookout Point, to east, has excellent winter view (partly obstructed in summer) of mountains to south. Possible campsite.	**11.0**
3.5	Cross old road. Trail curves here. Do not take old road. *Look for blazes.*	**10.6**
3.6	Cross branch of Spout Run. Blue-blazed trail 35 yd to south leads east 90 yd to intermittent *Sawmill Spring* and to **Sam Moore Shelter**. Northbound: Turn west and in 35 yd cross branch of Spout Run, ascending steeply.	**10.5**
4.0	Top of Tomblin Hill.	**10.1**

SECTION HIGHLIGHTS

Morgans Mill Rd – See "alternate access" information at beginning of section for trail access information, road directions, and parking availability.

Footbridge over Morgan Mill Stream   Ryan Day

N-S	TRAIL DESCRIPTION	
4.3	Cross old road in Fent Wiley Hollow, a broad, dark hollow with a great variety of mature trees.	**9.9**
4.5	Cross creek with two streams. Old still site is in woods to east.	**9.7**
4.6	Southbound: Turn west onto old road and ascend, very steeply at times.	**9.5**
5.0	Side trail to west leads past one rocky area to rocky summit of Buzzard Hill, with nice view to west (partially obscured in summer). A small, one-tent site is nearby, to south, on east side of *AT*.	**9.1**
5.3	Southbound: Bear westward onto old forest road. Northbound: Bear westward off old forest road and onto path, ascending first gradually and then very steeply.	**8.8**
5.6	Pass ruined foundation of old cabin on west side of Trail. Fifty yd south of this point is a *spring* on east side of Trail.	**8.5**
5.9	Southbound: Bear west at seasonal *spring* on east side of Trail and descend very steeply, with rocky footing.	**8.2**
6.0	Cross main creek in Reservoir Hollow; Acadia's Falls is 160 yd upstream.	**8.1**
6.8	Cross Va 605 (**Morgans Mill Rd**). *Watch for bees on north side in summer.*	**7.3**
7.0	Pass through outcrops. Slight southward view from rocks.	**7.1**
7.3	Cross footbridge over Morgan Mill Stream in Ashby Hollow. Hemlocks. Southbound: Cross dirt road still in use, and ascend lower north side of Piney Ridge Mtn, very steeply at times, through chestnut, oak and pine. Campsite on east side of *AT*.	**6.8**

S-N

Rod Hollow Shelter – Accommodates seven persons. It has a *spring*, privy, and sheltered picnic table and hearth, as well as four tent sites.

Rod Hollow Shelter   Henry Horn

N-S	TRAIL DESCRIPTION	
8.2	Knoll on Piney Ridge. View east.	**5.9**
8.8	Cross creek in Bolden Hollow. Southbound: Bear eastward as *AT* and ATV trail merge for about 125 yd., then turn west as series of switchbacks help ease 400-ft ascent of lower south side of Piney Ridge Mtn, to next peak	**5.3**
9.0	Cross ATV trail; keep straight.	**5.1**
9.3	Narrow, rocky ridge with limited view from rocky area 30 yd to west. Northbound: Trail follows series of switchbacks, some of which are old forest roads, in making 400-ft descent to Bolden Hollow.	**4.8**
10.1	300-foot boardwalk crosses wet area. Southbound: End of "The Roller Coaster." Northbound: Enter "The Roller Coaster" area as Trail ascends and descends numerous times to end of section.	**4.0**
10.2	Blue-blazed Fishers Hill Loop Trail to west ascends Fishers Hill and after 0.8 mi rejoins *AT* to south.	**3.9**
10.5	Blue-blazed trail to west leads 0.1 mi to **Rod Hollow Shelter** and *spring*. Old mine pits on both sides of Trail.	**3.6**
10.9	On ridge line, blue-blazed Fishers Hill Loop Trail to west ascends Fishers Hill and rejoins *AT* 0.8 mi to north.	**3.2**
11.0	Remains of stone wall.	**3.1**
11.3	Cross old stone wall; stream just to south in Duke Hollow.	**2.8**

Approach to Myron Glaser Cabin   Darrell Midgette

| **N-S** | TRAIL DESCRIPTION | |

11.8	Blue-blazed trail to west leads 0.2 mi to back side of Myron Glaser Cabin, reserved for PATC members only.	**2.3**
12.1	Cross creek (*not a dependable water source*).	**2.0**
12.3	Blue-blazed trail leads 0.2 mi west to Myron Glaser Cabin, reserved for PATC members only. *Side trail is hard to see southbound.*	**1.8**
12.7	Cross creek.	**1.5**
13.9	Blue-blazed trail leads east 85 yd to PATC trailhead parking lot; Trail crosses stream 25 yd to south.	**0.2**
14.1	Cross US 50 bearing slightly to west. Section ends at post in median strip of US 50, 0.25 mi west of Ashby Gap. Northbound: Enter woods and ascend through dense undergrowth, elms, and lots of dogwood.	**0.0**

AT Elevation Profile -- Virginia Section 4

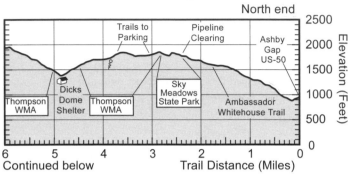

North end

Trails to Parking

Pipeline Clearing

Ashby Gap US-50

Dicks Dome Shelter

Sky Meadows State Park

Thompson WMA

Thompson WMA

Ambassador Whitehouse Trail

Elevation (Feet)

Trail Distance (Miles)

Continued below

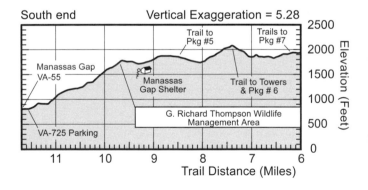

South end

Vertical Exaggeration = 5.28

Trail to Pkg #5

Trails to Pkg #7

Manassas Gap VA-55

Manassas Gap Shelter

Trail to Towers & Pkg # 6

G. Richard Thompson Wildlife Management Area

VA-725 Parking

Elevation (Feet)

Trail Distance (Miles)

SECTION 4
ASHBY GAP TO MANASSAS GAP
Distance: 11.8 Miles

As in Virginia Section 3, the *AT* in this section has been relocated onto publicly acquired land. As a consequence of these relocations, and because a road follows the ridge crest, the Trail now snakes along the slopes, dipping in and out of numerous ravines. Although the footing is generally good, these undulations make this a moderately difficult day hike. Much of the land in this section is part of the G. Richard Thompson Wildlife Management Area, which is under the jurisdiction of the Virginia Department of Game and Inland Fisheries. Hunters may pose a danger during season.

This section has excellent views from the open pasture areas on the US Park Service Ovoka Tract just north of Sky Meadows State Park. This part of the Ovoka Tract also has some odd rock formations. There are interesting rock outcrops at 9.9/1.7 mi. The *AT* in vicinity of 7.4/4.4 mi is noted for its profuse growth of trillium in early May. This section also has a great variety of flora: orchards, sapling forests, jungles of vines, and lots of wildflowers.

In Sky Meadows State Park, the Ambassador Whitehouse Trail leads to a view of Paris, Va. The *AT*, Ambassador Whitehouse Trail, Northern Ridge Trail, and the Old Trail form a network of trails providing loop hikes.

Road Access

Northern end of section at Ashby Gap: This is on US 50. The *AT* crosses US 50, 0.25 mi west of the gap. There is a PATC 10-car parking lot on the west side of Va 601, about 0.2 mile north of US 50 (NAD83 N39° 01.627', W77° 57.718'). A blue-blazed access trail at the back of the lot descends to the *AT* in 85 yd (at 13.9/0.2 in Section 3 description). Paris is 1.0 mile east and Washington, D.C., is 56 miles east.

Southern end of section at Manassas Gap: This is on Va 55, at Linden. The *AT* crosses Va 55 about a mile east of Linden, at the junction with Va 725. From the east, on I-66, exit onto Va 55 at Linden (exit 13). The *AT*, going north, follows Va 725. There is trailhead parking with room for 10 to 12 cars just off Va 725, 0.1 mile north of Va 55 junction (NAD83 N38° 84.686', W78° 03.163'). Markham is about 3.4 miles east, Front Royal is about 7.1 miles west, and Washington, D.C., is 65 miles away.

Alternate access to Trillium flowers in G. Richard Thompson Wildlife Management Area: From Va 55, at Manassas Gap, take Va 638 north for about five miles to Trillium parking area (NAD83 N38° 57.206', W78° 01.631'). There is room for 6 cars. From the parking area, follow the fire road past the gate for about 0.1 mile to a blue-blazed Trico Tower Trail on right that leads south 0.3 mile to the *AT* (at 7.4/4.4 mi), providing access for shorter hikes in this section.

Alternate access to other parking for the G. Richard Thompson Wildlife Management Area: From Va 55, at Manassas Gap, take Va 638 north approximately 4 miles to Upper Ted Lake parking area (NAD83 N38° 56.235', W78° 02.680'), on right. From this parking area blue-blazed Ted Lake Trail follows old road 0.8 mile from here to *AT* (at 9.3/2.5 mi). Next is the small unsigned Verlin Smith Parking (NAD83 N38° 56.385', W78° 02.380'). From this parking area Verlin Smith Trail follows a fire road 0.3 mile to *AT* (8.5/3.3 mi). Farther north on Va 638, unsigned parking area (old parking area #7) lies on the right at junction with Blue Mountain Road (NAD83 N38° 57.799', W78° 01.180'). A gated old road leads right (east) 0.2 mile from here to *AT* (at 6.3/5.7 mi). There are other parking areas farther north on gravel Fire Trail Road at the junction with Blue Mountain Road.

Access to Sky Meadows State Park: See section in *"Side Trails."*

Maps
PATC Map 8 and USGS Paris, Upperville, and Linden Quadrangles.

Shelters, Campsites, and Other Public Facilities
Sky Meadows State Park (1.3 mi by side trail, at 2.6/9.4 mi) has camping at designated sites and a shelter. Nightly fee per campsite is required (limited to six persons per site). See section on *"Side Trails."*

Dick's Dome Shelter (0.2 mi by side trail, at 4.9/6.9 mi), beside Whiskey Hollow Creek, accommodates four and is being replaced by the Whiskey Hollow Shelter.

Manassas Gap Shelter (70 yd by side trail, at 9.3/2.5 mi) accommodates six persons and has a *spring* nearby.

Supplies
A post office, and a small store are at the junction of Va 55 and Va 638, at Manassas Gap (Linden). Water is available from springs at 3.9/7.9 mi, at Manassas Gap Shelter, and from Sky Meadows State Park.

US Park Service Ovoka Tract – In 2003, the National Park Service added 445 acres of the historic and scenic Ovoka Farm to the *AT* corridor along the eastern side of the Blue Ridge Mountains between Ashby Gap and Sky Meadows State Park. The land was acquired through a transfer from the Piedmont Environmental Council and was funded by Congressional action sponsored by Senator John Warner and former Congressman Frank Wolf.

The property includes more than 100 acres of open fields that offer spectacular views of the lush farms, forests and stream of the Virginia Piedmont and of Loudoun Valley, Route 50 corridor, Lonesome Mountain, the village of Paris, Crocked Run Valley, and the Bull Run Mountains.

PATC volunteers relocated the *AT* onto the Ovoka Tract to take advantage of the open fields and views that offered a distinct change from the typical forest environment of the *AT* through this area. The relocated *AT* was officially opened in a ceremony on June 4, 2005. The ceremony featured remarks by former Congressman Frank Wolf, Appalachian Trail Park Office Superintendent, Piedmont Environmental Council President, and representatives from ATC, PATC, and Sky Meadows State Park. The ceremony concluded with Congressman Wolf releasing a red-tailed hawk rehabilitated by the Blue Ridge Wildlife Center.

Ambassador Whitehouse Trail – Leads 0.5 mile to the broad, grassy meadows of Sky Meadows State Park, with a view east of the valley and small town of Paris, VA. See section on "*Side Trails.*"

Old Trail – This is the old route of the *AT*, now blazed purple and designated Old Trail by Sky Meadows State Park. For more information see section on "*Side Trails.*"

N-S

TRAIL DESCRIPTION

0.0	Northern end of section at median strip of US 50, 0.25 mi west of Ashby Gap. Southbound: Cross US 50 bearing slightly right. Enter woods on path. Cross stone wall and turn right onto old roadbed. Northbound: Turn left and cross stone wall to US 50. To continue on Trail, cross US 50 and enter woods.	11.8
0.2	Trail turns sharply east and ascends.	11.6
0.7	Pass rock piles on east, in former cleared field covered in shrubs and vines.	11.1
0.9	Cross telephone cable right-of-way.	10.9
1.1	Junction with **Old Trail** (purple blaze). Bear east.	10.7
1.2	Cross old roadbed, marking northern boundary of **US Park Service Ovoka Tract**. Northbound: After road crossing, descend through woods.	10.6
1.4	Open pasture.	10.4
1.6	Pass through lightly wooded area bounded by open pasture.	10.2
1.8	Junction with **Ambassador Whitehouse Trail** on east. Southbound: Bear west onto old roadbed. Northbound: Bear west at junction and continue through pasture.	10.0
2.3	Southbound: Ascend to level, lightly wooded pasture. Northbound: Descend on old roadbed through woods.	9.5

Sky Meadows State Park – The 1,862 acre Sky Meadows State Park (for details see "Side Trail" or Park's website at http://www.dcr. virginia.gov/state_parks/sky.shtml) offers a campground (0.75 mi from the Visitor Center parking lot) and some short circuit hikes with extraordinary views from the Park's high meadows. The Park is open from 8 a.m. to dusk daily and has a small entrance fee per car. **Sky Meadows State Park Visitor Center** is located beside the parking lot. The Visitor Center (open year round) has restrooms available year-round.

Sky Meadows State Park Campground – Has tent pads at several sites, fire pits, pit toilets, and a hand-pump well (*water* ***must*** be boiled or disinfected, however). AT thru hiker site is located just below hand-pump well and is marked as such. The camping fee is $15 per site (payment instructions are located at the site) with a limit of six persons per site. Reservations are recommended. Campers must arrive before the Park closes at dusk. Camping and fires are prohibited elsewhere in the Park. For more information see section on "Side Trails." *Special procedures apply if you wish to park overnight in the Visitor Center parking. Call 540-592-3556 for details.*

Signal Knob – Signal Knob was the site of a Civil War signal station.

N-S | TRAIL DESCRIPTION

2.5	Cross gas pipeline right-of-way, marking southern limit of **US Park Service Ovoka Tract** and northern boundary of **Sky Meadows State Park.** Just south of the pipeline right-of-way is a junction with **Old Trail** (purple-blazed) on west. Northbound: Pass through lightly wooded pasture.	**9.3**
2.6	Blue-blazed North Ridge Trail on east leads 1.7 mi to **Sky Meadows State Park Visitors Center**, or 1.3 mi to **Sky Meadows State Park campground**. See section on *"Side Trails."*	**9.2**
2.9	Northern boundary of **G. Richard Thompson State Wildlife Management Area**. Southbound: *AT* passes through the Management Area for most of next 7.3 mi. Hunters may pose a danger during season.	**8.9**
3.1	Pass path, on west side of Trail, leading 0.1 mi to 10-car Orchard parking area.	**8.7**
3.6	Southbound: Enter overgrown clearing with dense vines and shrubs. Trail blazed on poles. Northbound: Enter woods and descend on path, then ascend.	**8.2**
3.7	Spur trail on west leads 0.1 mi to Appalachian Trail named parking area for 10 cars on **Signal Knob**. Continue straight. Southbound: South of spur trail, enter woods. Northbound: Bear east, with overgrown view to south and southeast.	**8.1**
3.9	Pass *spring* on east side of Trail. Trail continues on old roadbed under canopy of vines and shrubs. Northbound: Enter large overgrown clearing with heavy growth of vines and shrubs.	**7.9**

S-N

SECTION HIGHLIGHTS

G. Richard Thompson State Wildlife Management Area – This area is under the jurisdiction of the Virginia Department of Game and Inland Fisheries (DGIF). Approximately 7.3 mi of the Trail pass through this management area. Hunters may pose a danger during hunting season. The area is described on the DGIF website as: *Situated within a convenient distance of Northern Virginia's large, urban population but far removed in its setting – against the quiet eastern slope of the Blue Ridge Mountains – the G. Richard Thompson Wildlife Management Area is among the most popular of the Game Department lands. The opportunities to hunt, fish, view wildlife and the spectacular displays of wildflowers, or hike a stretch of the famous Appalachian Trail, contribute to the area's broad appeal."*

The Virginia Department of Game and Inland Fisheries (DGIF) require an Access Permit for visitors to department-owned Wildlife Management Areas. Access Permit fees are waived and no application for a waiver needs to be submitted for individuals hiking on the Appalachian Trail or Great Eastern Trail and for Appalachian Trail maintenance workers/crews while engaged in maintenance work on the Trail.

Dick's Dome Shelter – Reached by going 0.2 mi by side trail, at 4.9/6.9 mi. Located beside Whiskey Hollow Creek, accommodates four. Privy on hillside a short distance above. Drinking water from the creek is not advisable without treating. PATC member Dick George built this shelter on private land for *AT* hikers. The land was later transferred to the NPS. The shelter is being replaced by the new Whiskey Hollow Shelter.

4.4 Road and path meet at boundary of Game   **7.4**
Commission land. Southbound: Turn right, off road
and onto path, entering land purchased for Trail by
State of Virginia. Descend steeply. Northbound:
Turn west onto old road, re-entering G. R. Thompson
WMA.

4.8 Cross dirt road.   **7.0**

4.9 Cross creek in Whiskey Hollow, at boundary of G.   **6.9**
R. Thompson WMA. Blue-blazed trail on east, 70 yd
south of creek, leads 0.2 mi to **Dick's Dome Shelter**.
Southbound: Ascend steeply by switchbacks, re-
entering G. R. Thompson WMA. Northbound:
Enter US Park Service *AT* corridor. Ascend.

5.5 Pass lone boulder. Southbound: Ascend more   **6.3**
moderately. Northbound: Descend very steeply.

6.0 Reach level crest.   **5.8**

6.1 Northbound: Bear east onto old road. Level, then   **5.7**
descend.

6.3 Small clearing. To west, road leads 0.2 mi to unsigned   **5.5**
parking area and Va 638. Southbound: Just ahead,
cross old road then small clearing. Northbound:
Cross small clearing then old road.

7.1 Southbound: Turn east onto dirt road (Trico Road),   **4.7**
then almost immediately turn west off road and
ascend very steeply. To west, Trico Road leads 0.7 mi
to Trillium parking area and Va 638. Northbound:
Turn west onto dirt road (Trico Road), then almost
immediately turn east off road and descend.

SECTION HIGHLIGHTS

Manassas Gap Shelter – Located 70 yd by side trail, at 9.3/2.5 mi, accommodates six persons and has a *spring* nearby.

Log cabin at Sky Meadows State Park   Laurie Potteiger

N-S	TRAIL DESCRIPTION	

7.4 Blue-blazed Trico Tower Trail (aka Trillium Trail) leads west 0.3 mi to Trico Road just short of Trillium parking area and Va 638. Northbound: Descend very steeply. **4.4**

8.1 Cross intermittent stream. Southbound: Ascend ahead. Northbound: Trail ascends, then becomes level ahead. **3.7**

8.5 Turn east onto dirt road (Verlin Smith Trail). Road leads west 0.4 mi to Verlin Smith unsigned parking area and Va 638. Southbound: In 90 yd, turn west off road. Northbound: In 90 yd, Trail veers to east. **3.3**

9.3 Crossroads. To west, DGIF Ted Lake Trail leads 0.8 mi to Upper Ted Lake parking area and Va 638. Just north of crossroads, blue-blazed trail leads east 70 yd to **Manassas Gap Shelter** and *spring*. Southbound: Turn east at crossroads. Go 90 yd and turn west into woods. Ascend through hickory, sassafras, oak, yellow poplar. Northbound: Turn east at cross roads, Ted Lake Trail continues straight. After junction with blue-blazed trail to Manassas Gap Shelter, ascend steeply. **2.5**

9.8 Boundary of **G. Richard Thompson Wildlife Management Area**. Southbound: Leave management area and descend, passing dense undergrowth and dogwood. Northbound: Enter management area. The *AT* passes through the Management Area for most of the next 7.3 mi. Hunters may pose a danger during season. Trail undulates ahead around left side of knob. **2.0**

| SECTION HIGHLIGHTS |

Linden – Located in Manassas Gap, is about 1.0 mi to west on Route 55. It has a post office, small store, and telephone at junction with Va 638. Also at junction is **Discovery Monument**, commemorating the supposed site from which John Lederer, nurse and explorer, first saw the Shenandoah Valley in 1670. He came to this country from Germany in 1669 and was part of the first group of Europeans to see the Blue Ridge.

NPS Ovoka Tract–Ambassador White House Trail   Laurie Potteiger

N-S	TRAIL DESCRIPTION	
9.9	Trail passes between interesting rock formations. Monolithic outcrops jut up from ground.	**1.9**
10.1	Old stone wall on east. Continue to descend/ascend through rocky areas.	**1.7**
10.8	Blue-blazed trail leads east to overgrown view from hillside.	**1.0**
10.9	Switchbacks, with stone steps at south end. Southbound: Descend. Northbound: Ascend.	**0.9**
11.2	Cross small open area. Southbound: After open area, turn west then east and climb up wooden steps. Northbound: Wooden steps. Cross old farm lane, turn east then west to reach open area.	**0.6**
11.4	Top of small ridge.	**0.4**
11.6	Northbound: Turn right off Va 725 and cross PATC trailhead parking lot. Cross substantial footbridge with steel girders built to withstand heavy spring runoff (bridge replaced by Eagle Scout project in 2007).	**0.2**
11.8	Southern end of section near **Linden** in Manassas Gap. Southbound: Intersect Va 55 after passing under I-66 overpasses. To continue on Trail, cross Va 55 and enter woods to right of junction. Northbound: Junction of Va 55 and Va 725. Follow Va 725, passing under I-66 overpasses.	**0.0**

AT Elevation Profile -- Virginia Section 5

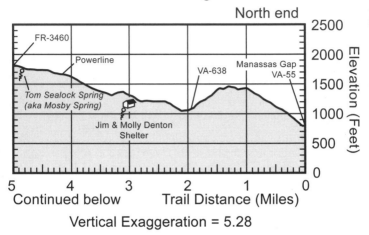

Vertical Exaggeration = 5.28

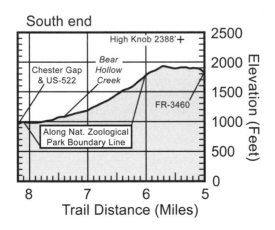

SECTION 5
MANASSAS GAP TO CHESTER GAP
Distance: 8.2 Miles

From either direction, this section poses a nearly 1,000-foot ascent along the slopes of High Knob and a 600-foot ascent of a neighboring mountain. The ascents are somewhat steeper from the south. The footing is generally good. The highlight of this section is a former pasture on top of a mountain with outstanding views in several directions (at 1.2/6.9 mi). This section can be combined with Virginia Section 6 for a moderate day hike, if hiked from south to north.

Road Access

Northern end of section near Manassas Gap: This is on Va 55, at Linden. The *AT* crosses Va 55 about 1.0 mile east of Linden, at the junction with Va 725. From the east, on I-66, exit onto Va 55 at Markham. From the west, on I-66, get onto Va 55 at the Linden exit. The *AT*, going south, enters the woods just a few yards west of the junction. There is room for several cars to park by the junction (NAD83 N38° 54.554', W78° 03.196'). Markham is about 3.4 miles east, Front Royal is about 7.1 miles west, and Washington, D.C., is about 65 miles away.

Alternate access via Va 725: There is trailhead parking with room for 10 to 12 cars just off Va 725, 0.1 mile north of Va 55 junction (NAD83 N38° 54.681', W78° 03.163').

Alternate access via Va 638: There is limited parking at gate west of crossing of Va 638 (NAD83 N38° 53.862', W78° 04.307').

Southern end of section at US 522 near Chester Gap: The *AT* crosses this highway at a point 1.5 miles west of Chester Gap and 3.2 miles east of Va 55, in Front Royal. There is room for several cars to park on the south side of the highway at the *AT* crossing (NAD83 N38° 52.674', W78° 09.042').

Maps

PATC Map 8 and USGS Linden and Front Royal Quadrangles.

Shelters, Campsites, and Other Public Facilities

The Jim and Molly Denton Shelter (50 yd by side trail, at 3.0/5.2 mi) accommodates 7 persons under the roof and has a large porch with a wooden bench. Other facilities include privy, *spring*, shower, covered picnic table, fireplace, and limited tent sites.

Mosby Campsite (100 yd by side trail, at 4.9/3.3 mi) has benches, several places for tents and a nearby *spring*, but no other facilities.

Supplies

A small store is at the junction of Va 55 and Va 638, at Manassas Gap (Linden). A post office is located just east of the junction on north side of Va 55.

Water is available from a *spring*, at 3.0/5.2 mi, and from *Tom Sealock Spring* (125 yd by side trail, at 4.9/3.3 mi).

SECTION HIGHLIGHTS

Linden – Nearby, at the junction of Va 55 and Va 638 (about 1.0 mi to west on level route). Located in Manassas Gap, Linden has a post office and small store at junction of Va 55 and Va 638.

Discovery Monument – Located at the junction of Va 55 and Va 638, commemorates the supposed site from which John Lederer, nurse and explorer, first saw the Shenandoah Valley in 1670.

Old orchard – Part of an open pasture. There is a good view of High Knob.

Cleared field – Superb winter view on west, through gap, of Shenandoah Valley and the West Virginia mountains beyond. Excellent view down Trumbo Hollow from top of hill.

N-S	TRAIL DESCRIPTION	

0.0	Northern end of section at junction of Va 55 and Va 725 near **Linden**, which is the location of the **Discovery Monument**. Southbound: Enter woods through weedy area to right of junction. Ahead, a bridge and boardwalk Cross several channels of Goose Creek. Northbound: cross Va 55 and follow Va 725.	**8.2**
0.1	Cross railroad tracks. Southbound: Ascend steeply. Northbound: Beyond, a bridge and boardwalk cross several channels of Goose Creek.	**8.1**
0.5	Cross faint old road. Southbound: Turn west onto old road at junction. Go east at fork in a few yd.	**7.7**
0.7	Base of large cliff. Steep switchbacks both directions. Northbound: After switchbacks, go straight onto old road, which intersects from west, and then turn west, off road and onto path, in a few yd.	**7.5**
0.8	Boulder area with overgrown **orchard** to the south. Southbound: Switchback to right over boulders, enter old orchard and go straight. Northbound: Turn west off road and cross overgrown orchard, enter woods, and descend ahead over boulders.	**7.2**
1.1	White-blazed posts. Southbound: Turn west onto old, sunken road and follow white-blazed posts. Northbound: Enter **cleared field** of former pasture on mountain top. Cross center of field and descend. Follow white-blazed posts.	**7.1**
1.2	Cross center of **cleared field** of former pasture on mountain top. Southbound: Bear slightly west from center to next post. Northbound: Descend and follow white-blazed posts.	**7.0**

John McDowell

Jim and Molly Denton Shelter

TRAIL DESCRIPTION

1.3 Cross over crest of ridge, not along it, through an old field that is becoming overgrown. Descend ahead. View of High Knob from southern side, looking south. **6.9**

1.6 Old road. Southbound: Turn west and descend on old road. Northbound: Turn east onto old road and ascend then turn west off road. **6.6**

1.7 Pass on east side of corral. Southbound: Bear left off road at edge of former farm. Go around left side of corral. Descend through pasture toward Va 638. **6.5**

1.9 Paved Va 638. Southbound: Before reaching Va 638, pass through fence next to gate. Turn east onto paved Va 638. *Watch for traffic.* In about 30 yd, turn west off road. Northbound: Turn west onto paved Va 638. *Watch for traffic.* In about 30 yd, turn east off road. Beyond, pass through fence next to gate. **6.3**

2.1 Cross over small stream. **6.1**

2.2 Intersection with another trail. Northbound: Turn east where trail intersects. *AT* then goes west and begins to descend steeply. **6.0**

2.5 Southbound: Turn west, leaving path that follows ridge crest. **5.7**

2.6 Cross old stone wall. **5.6**

2.9 Old road intersects on west. Southbound: Go straight. Northbound: Go east at fork. **5.3**

SECTION HIGHLIGHTS

Denton Shelter – The Jim and Molly Denton Shelter (50 yd by side trail, at 3.0/5.2 mi) accommodates 7 persons under the roof and has a large porch with a wooden bench. Other facilities include privy, *spring*, shower, covered picnic table, fireplace, and limited tent sites.

Jim and Molly Denton were active members of PATC from 1960-1991. They lived in Front Royal so that the mountains of northern Virginia and the Shenandoah were in their backyard. For many years they edited the *AT Guide to Shenandoah National Park with Side Trails,* and the *Circuit Hikes in Shenandoah National Park.* This shelter was built as a memorial to their years of dedicated volunteer work for PATC and the hiking community.

Mosby Campsite – Primitive campsite site on ten acres of land donated to the PATC in 1965 by Mrs. Mary H. Keyser. PATC donated the land to the National Park Service in 1987. A former shelter on this site was apparently stolen in 1980 for the sake of its chestnut logs.

Tom Sealock Spring – Named for one of Col. Mosby's men, who lived here after the Civil War. The spring is at the Mosby Campsite.

TRAIL DESCRIPTION

3.0 Trail on west leads 50 yd to **Denton Shelter** and campground. The spring trail is 100 yards south of the shelter trail.   **5.2**

3.1 Southbound: Turn west, off road and onto path, and descend briefly. Lots of hickory, including shagbark, and yellow poplar throughout area. Northbound: Turn west onto road.   **5.1**

3.7 Base of small cliff. To north, lots of hickory, including shagbark, and yellow poplar.   **4.5**

4.2 Cross parallel 500KV powerline right-of-way. Fair view to west.   **4.0**

4.6 Old road. Southbound: Follow old roadbed. Northbound: Leave old roadbed.   **3.6**

4.7 Old road. Northbound: Turn east and immediately turn west onto old roadbed. Southbound: Turn west off old roadbed, then turn east.   **3.5**

4.9 Cross stream. Spotted touch-me-nots have been seen in the past in this area. At 70 yd north of stream, blue-blazed trail leads east 100 yd to **Mosby Campsite** (primitive) and another 25 yd downhill to *Tom Sealock Spring*.   **3.3**

5.0 Cross Forest Road 3460 (old CCC Road).   **3.2**

5.1 Southbound: Turn west onto old road. Northbound: Turn west off road and onto path.   **3.1**

5.4 Southbound: Turn east off road and descend very steeply with rocky footing. Northbound: Turn east onto road.   **2.8**

SECTION HIGHLIGHTS

Smithsonian Conservation Biology Institute (SCBI) – The Institute is a 4,000-acre wildlife preserve belonging to the National Zoological Park, an agency of the Smithsonian Institution. The land was formerly a USDA livestock research station and, before that, a U.S. Cavalry remount post. A World War II prisoner-of-war camp was at the top of the ridge, above the former cavalry remount post. An easement for the *AT* passes over the SCBI land. *Camping and hunting are prohibited.*

Old stone wall   Catherine Kelleher

N-S	TRAIL DESCRIPTION	

5.7	Area of steep ascents and descents with rocky footing.	2.5
5.9	Northern boundary of **SCBI**. *Camping and hunting are prohibited from here to southern end of section.*	2.3
6.2	Fork. Southbound: Go west at fork. Northbound: Bear west.	2.0
6.3	Cross maintenance road. Gate to zoo is on west.	1.9
6.4	Cross old road. Southbound: Turn right onto the old road and ahead turn left off road and onto path.	1.8
6.8	Area of dense undergrowth periodically. Trail goes along fence of Conservation and Research Center.	1.4
7.4	Cross Bear Hollow Creek.	0.8
7.9	Near fence corner, follow maintenance road toward highway. Zoo gate is on west. Southbound: Trail turns west just short of highway and parallels highway between old fence and highway. View of Lake Front Royal across highway. Northbound: Continue on grassy old road, between fence and Bear Hollow Creek.	0.3
8.2	Southern end of section at US 522 near Chester Gap. Southbound: Turn east, and reach US 522. To continue on Trail, cross US 522. Northbound: Ascend embankment and turn east as Trail parallels highway between old fence and highway. Enter land of **SCBI**. *Camping and hunting are prohibited on the SCBI land (next 2.3 mi).* Pass through scrub ahead, with view of Lake Front Royal across highway.	0.0

AT Elevation Profile -- Virginia Section 6

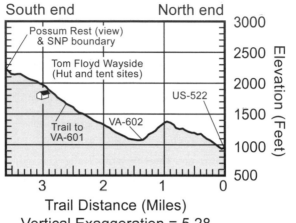

Trail Distance (Miles)
Vertical Exaggeration = 5.28

SECTION 6
CHESTER GAP TO
SHENANDOAH NATIONAL PARK
Distance: 3.6 Miles

From north to south, this section has 1,600 feet of ascent and only 300 feet of descent. The footing is very good. This section can be combined with Virginia Section 5 for a moderate day hike, if hiked from south to north. There are two good views (at 1.7/1.9 mi, and 3.6/0.0 mi). The variety of growth is also interesting.

Road Access

Northern end of section near Chester Gap: AT crosses US 522 at a point 1.5 miles west of Chester Gap and 3.2 miles east of Va 55, in Front Royal (NAD83 N38° 52.674', W78° 09.042'). There is room for several cars to park on the south side of the highway.

Alternate access via Va 602 or Va 601:   From US 522, between Front Royal and the *AT* crossing, take paved Va 604 south. Graveled Va 602 forks to the left; room for two cars to park (NAD83 N38° 51.842', W78° 09.746'). Farther ahead on Va 604, graveled Va 601 forks to the left. Va 601 has a parking area (on PATC land) on the right, marked by a sign, with room for about four cars (NAD83 N38° 51.309', W78° 10.348'). A blue-blazed access trail, opposite, ascends 0.7 mi to the *AT*.

Alternate access at Shenandoah National Park Boundary: From US 522, turn onto crescent-shaped road on south side of Chester Gap. Turn onto Va 610 and follow it to Park boundary (NAD83 N38° 50.943', W78° 09.110'). There is room for several cars to park here. Continue on foot up dirt road (old Compton Gap Road) for 0.5 mi. Then turn right onto *AT* and descend another 0.2 mi to Park boundary, at southern end of Section 6.

Maps

PATC Map 9 and USGS Front Royal and Chester Gap Quadrangles.

Shelters, Campsites, and Other Public Facilities

Tom Floyd Wayside (short distance by side trail, at 2.9/0.7 mi) has shelter and lies 0.2 mi uphill from *Ginger Spring*. Use is free on a first-come, first-served basis. *Camp fires and group camping are prohibited.* Users must carry out all trash. Shenandoah National Park backcountry permits are available from a self-serve kiosk just inside the park boundary. Northern Virginia 4-H Educational Center (0.3 mi west of *AT* at 1.4/2.2) has *water* available April - October and a pool open Memorial Day to Labor Day (admission: $4).

Supplies

Water is available from *Ginger Spring* (0.2 mi by side trail, at 2.6/1.0 mi).

SECTION HIGHLIGHTS

Smithsonian Conservation Biology Institute (SCBI) – The Institute is a 4,000-acre wildlife preserve belonging to the National Zoological Park, an agency of the Smithsonian Institution. The land was formerly a USDA livestock research station and, before that, a U.S. Cavalry remount post. *Camping and hunting are prohibited.* A World War II prisoner-of-war camp was at the top of the ridge, above the former cavalry remount post.

Northern Virginia 4-H Educational Center – *Water* available April - October; pool open Memorial. Day to Labor Day. Admission: $4. The Center offers accommodations for conferences and retreats. Its programs include challenge courses, environmental education, outdoor education, and a camp for children with cancer.

N-S	TRAIL DESCRIPTION	

0.0	Northern end of section near Chester Gap, at US 522. Cross 270-foot boardwalk over marshy area. Southbound: Trail ahead follows National Park Service easement over land belonging to the **SCBI**. Northbound: To continue on Trail, cross US 522 and ascend embankment.	**3.6**
0.1	Southbound: Ascend ridge, steeply at times, with fenced meadow and good view on west. Ticks are common in this area. Frequent inspections for ticks are recommended.	**3.5**
0.5	Edge of woods, dominated by tulip poplar trees. Northbound: Descend ridge, steeply at times, with fenced meadow and good view on west. Ticks are common in this area. Frequent inspections for ticks are recommended	**3.1**
0.7	Cross ditch. Evening orchids may be seen beside large tulip tree on north side of ditch.	**2.9**
0.9	Cross crest of spur ridge and descend. Forest dominated by tulip poplar.	**2.7**
1.4	Cross Va 602, 50 yd north of Moore Run crossing. *Do not take water from Moore Run*, for there are houses upstream. Reach **Northern Virginia 4-H Educational Center** by going 0.3 mi west, then turning up an uphill driveway. Beech trees dominate forested land south of VA 602, owned by Virginia Tech.	**2.2**
1.5	Cross intermittent stream. Do not take water from stream because of houses upstream.	**2.1**
1.7	Pass through previous open area now covered with scrub and vines.	**1.9**

SECTION HIGHLIGHTS

Tom Floyd Wayside Shelter – Facilities include shelter, 5 tent sites, and *Ginger Spring*. Three separate blue-blazed trails (2.6/1.0 mi, 2.8/0.8 mi, and 2.9/0.7 mi) lead from *AT*, through extensive growth of white ash and tulip trees, to shelter.

Tom Floyd Wayside   John McDowell

N-S	TRAIL DESCRIPTION	

1.8	Southbound: Enter woods again. Northbound: Leave woods.	1.8
1.9	Giant beech on west among forest of oak, hickory, and sassafras.	1.7
2.1	Blue-blazed trail (old *AT*) bears east. Trail leads west to **Northern Virginia 4-H Center**.	1.5
2.2	Cross powerline	1.4
2.6	Blue-blazed trail on west side of *AT* leads to Va 601 and PATC parking lot. (Travel downhill 0.3 mi to sharp turn at VA 601; trail veers right along old roadbed for about 50 yd before turning left into woods, then continues 0.4 mi before rejoining Va 601 opposite PATC lot.) Just ahead is one of three spur trails leading west into **Tom Floyd Wayside Shelter**, tent sites, and *Ginger Spring*. A strong aroma of sassafras may be detectable in places.	1.0
2.8	Blue-blazed trail on west leads 0.2 mi to *Ginger Spring* and tent site #1, built for shelter overflow. Branches of this trail lead uphill to tent site #2 and to **Tom Floyd Wayside Shelter**.	0.8
2.9	Blue-blazed trail on west leads to **Tom Floyd Wayside Shelter**. This side trail continues past shelter to overflow tent sites and downhill to *Ginger Spring*.	0.7
3.3	Ridge crest.	0.3
3.4	Cross old road and ascend.	0.2
3.5	Southbound: Ascend steeply up cliff. Northbound: Bottom of cliff. Descend ahead through oak and hickory forest	0.1

S-N

Possum Rest – 180-degree view west from top of cliff. Trail in this area is within the Harmony Hollow scenic easement, first such easement established in Virginia.

6/06/07 11:21 AM

Mega-Transect camera   PATC

The SCBI in Luray, VA, is partnering with the National Park Service, Appalachian Trail Conservancy and PATC to maintain 50 infrared, motion-dectection cameras along the AT in VA, WV, MD and southern PA to record mammal activity. Cameras are set up off-trail and relocated to a new site every month from April 1 to October 31. A scent is used to attract mammals to the camera location. It is the ultimate intent of this monitoring program to produce long-term statistics in mammalian populations along the total length of the AT from GA to ME. This program is being conducted as a function of ATC's Mega-Transect initiative.

N-S

| TRAIL DESCRIPTION |

3.6 Southern end of section at boundary of Shenandoah National Park. Park backcountry permits are available from a self-serve kiosk just inside boundary. **Possum Rest** is 50 yd north of the park boundary, on *AT*. Chester Gap access trail junction with *AT* lies 0.2 mi south. Northbound: Turn east and descend cliff steeply.

0.0

SIDE TRAILS

MARYLAND

Bear Spring Cabin Trail
Distance: 1.0 Mile

Map
Cross-reference: Maryland *AT* Section 5.

The PATC maintains a number of blue-blazed side trails that either intersect or parallel the *AT*. They are noted in trail descriptions for each section. Most of these are short paths leading to shelters, or viewpoints, and do not require further description. The following trails, however, deserve a detailed description because of their particular features and/ or the access to the *AT* that they provide.

The approximately 220-mile Tuscarora Trail provides a loop to the west of the *AT*. It intersects the *AT* at Blue Mountain, Pennsylvania, and in the northern section of Shenandoah National Park. Separate guidebooks to this trail have been published by the PATC and the Keystone Trails Association.

There are also numerous side trails in the Catoctin Mountains and in the Washington, D.C. suburbs, but these too are covered in separate guidebooks published by the PATC.

Road Access
Access: From US Alt-40, take Marker Rd (or take Bolivar Rd, or Reno Monument Rd, to Marker Rd) and turn onto Mountain Church Rd. Turn right onto road beside Locust Valley First Church of God. Park in church parking lot. Parking is for cabin use only, not for day hiking.

From US 340, take Md 17 north. Turn left onto Main Street in Burkittsville. Then turn right onto Mountain Church Rd. Continue to left turn at Church Rd and see above.

Detailed Trail Data – From Road

0.0   Junction beside church. Walk around gate and ascend woods road past house. Note: Permission has been granted to pass through this private property to access cabin.

0.2   Pass pond on left, as road curves sharply to right.

0.3   Turn left off road and cross creek, reaching Bear Spring Cabin. Trail continues up hollow.

0.5   *Bear Spring*. Ascend more steeply ahead.

0.8   White Rocks Trail (see below) intersects on right. Continue ahead on woods road.

1.0   Junction with *AT*.

Detailed Trail Data – From *AT*

0.0   Junction with *AT*. Descend steeply.

0.2   White Rocks Trail (see below) intersects on left.

0.5   *Bear Spring*. Descend more gradually.

0.7   Bear Spring Cabin. Bear to right of cabin, cross creek, and turn right onto woods road.

0.8   As road curves sharply to left, pass pond on right.

1.0   Walk around gate to junction with Mountain Church Rd, beside Locust Valley First Church of God.

White Rocks Trail
Distance: 0.2 Mile

Map
Cross-reference: Maryland Section 5 and Bear Spring Cabin Trail.

Warning: White Rocks Trail ascends 310 feet elevation in just 0.23 mi. Due to the rough, uneven footing and steepness of the climb, the trail is not recommended for small children. The easier access to White Rocks, if hiking from the cabin, is to continue 0.2 mi farther uphill on the Bear Spring Cabin Trail (an elevation gain of 110 feet) and turn right on the *AT*. Go 0.5 mi along the gentle grade of the *AT* to White Rocks Cliff.

Detailed Trail Data

0.0   Junction with Bear Spring Cabin Trail. Ascend gradually to foot of quartzite cliff, then scramble very steeply up rocks. *Slippery at all times.*

0.2   Junction with *AT* at White Rocks Cliff. View from very small outcrop is fair in summer, but excellent in winter. The prominent ridge in view is South Mountain. This directional illusion is result of Lambs Knoll being offset to east from line of ridge.

Maryland Heights Trails
Distance: 4.7 Miles

These trails are located in the Maryland section of Harpers Ferry National Historical Park, at the southern end of Elk Ridge, across the Potomac from Harpers Ferry. The trails are outstanding for their natural beauty and historic features (see history below). Although relatively short, the trails contain substantial climbs and descents. *Park regulations prohibit camping and fires.* Rock climbers, but not hikers, are required to register with park rangers in Harpers Ferry.

Map
Cross-reference: Maryland *AT* Section 7.

Road Access
Two free parking areas exist on Sandy Hook Rd, within 0.2 mi of the trailhead. For access from Harpers Ferry, cross Goodloe Byron Memorial Footbridge and turn left onto canal towpath. Cross footbridge over canal and cross Sandy Hook Rd. *Watch out for traffic.* Trail starts here at old road. Distance from *AT* is 0.4 mi.

History Along the Trail
Elk Ridge was settled during the Revolutionary War by Scottish, German, and English immigrants. They were shepherds, gardeners, and weavers by trade, and they earned a living here by truck gardening and charcoal burning for the local iron furnaces. Gradually most of them migrated to the valleys to be closer to other employment. The last settlers were evacuated during the Civil War. Most of Elk Ridge was included in Samples Manor, a timber holding for charcoal. A narrow-gauge railroad ran along the ridge from near the Stone Fort to Solomons Gap. The horsedrawn coal carts were reversed on a turntable in Solomons Gap, where the charcoal was shipped by wagons to Antietam. Coking coal shipped by the Chesapeake & Ohio Canal replaced charcoal at the Antietam Ironworks in the late 1840s, and the rail line was abandoned.

The trails pass over a portion of Elk Ridge known as Maryland Heights, which played an important role in the Civil War. When Lee invaded Maryland in 1862, he detailed Jackson to capture Harpers Ferry. Maryland Heights was abandoned after a short fight by Federal Col. Thomas H. Ford, who was later court-martialed. From these heights, Confederate Major General R. H. Anderson bombarded Harpers Ferry. The garrison surrendered after a short siege, September 13-15.

There are numerous points of historical interest along the trail, mostly on the eastern side of the loop. "Six-Gun Battery" was composed of six 30-pound Parrott siege guns and two 24-pound howitzers. Nearby is the site of the house where Col. Ford made his decision to evacuate Federal troops from the ridge. Farther ahead is "100-Pound Gun." This gun was mounted on a circular track, and Federal gunners once fired it at a stone school house four miles away, demolishing the structure and killing several Confederates within. The Stone Fort on top of the ridge is constructed of large, shaped blocks of unmortared stone. It was built after 1862 as the anchor to the new Harpers Ferry defense system, and was to be the final refuge for the garrison in the event of another attack. There are parallel walls across the ridge, siege gun positions, three magazines, and low, outer stone walls to protect the infantry.

To the northwest, Bakerton and Martinsburg, W.Va., may be seen on clear days. To the east are Pleasant Valley and South Mountain. The signal station for communication with Washington, via Sugar Loaf Mountain and the widow's walk on the Emory house in Brightwood, is believed to have been located on a high point to the right of the trail. Albert D. Richardson (*Tales of the Secret Service*, 1865) tells of climbing to the signal station and fortifications with a pack train to supply water to troops. The history of this area is explained on plaques along the trails.

Detailed Trail Data

0.0   Sandy Hook Rd. Walk around gate and ascend on green-blazed Military Road trail.

0.6   Junction with un-blazed Naval Battery side trail. Turn right onto side trail (green-blazed Military Road trail turns left). Naval

Battery, built in May 1862, on right. Large earthworks for gun emplacements ahead. Pass pit on right, a "Powder Magazine."

0.7   Rejoin green-blazed Military Road trail.

0.8   Junction with western end of blue-blazed Stone Fort loop trail on left and red-blazed Overlook Cliff trail on right. Turn right on Overlook Cliff trail.

1.0   Junction with eastern end of blue-blazed Stone Fort loop trail. (You will return to this trail after visting Overlook Cliff). Descend steeply on red-blazed Overlook Cliff trail, passing unmarked trail on left.

1.4   Cliffs with outstanding view of Harpers Ferry, railroads and C&O Canal, and Potomac and Shenandoah Rivers. Return back up trail.

1.8   Turn right on blue-blazed Stone Fort loop trail.

2.0   Six-gun battery. Visit battery, then return to blue-blazed trail and continue.

2.4   Pass 100-pound gun battery, with excellent view of Potomac River and mountain ranges.

2.8   Reach Stone Fort. Cross wall of fort left of plaque. Ahead, bear left past faint trail ending in woods.

2.9   Pass interior fort, then descend down log steps to exterior fort.

3.1   Pass Civil War campgrounds.

3.5   Pass charcoal-making exhibit.

3.9   Reach end of blue-blazed Stone Fort loop trail, and rejoin green-blazed Military Road trail. Turn right and descend on green-blazed trail.

4.7   Reach Sandy Hook Rd.

CATOCTIN TRAIL
28.7 miles; 2.1 mi connector to *AT*

The Catoctin Trail (*CT*) is a rugged 28.7-mile, blue-blazed hiking trail that passes primarily through mature hardwood forests. It most often is hiked south to north. The segment descriptions below are arranged to reflect this preference. The *CT*'s southern terminus is in Gambrill State Park. From there it travels northward through the Frederick Municipal Watershed, Cunningham Falls State Park and Catoctin Mountain Park. Its northern terminus is at Mt. Zion Road, just beyond the boundary of Catoctin Mountain Park. From that point the Appalachian Trail is less than two miles away via an easy road walk.

The *CT* was constructed between 1979 and 1982 by the Potomac Appalachian Trail Club. It was designed primarily for day hiking with many easy access points. At this time (2015) camping and backpacker overnighting is permitted only in established campgrounds and inside cabins noted below (see "*Shelters, Campsites, and Other Public Facilities*").

In Gambrill State Park and the watersheds, the *CT* is shared with mountain bikes and horses. The northernmost 3 miles are a horse and foot trail. Hunting is popular on the land the *CT* traverses, especially in the watersheds, and is permitted within some park lands. Information on hunting season and territories is available at www.dnr.state.md.us/huntersguide. The *CT* occasionally crosses and borders private property, and respectful use of such property is important.

The entire *CT* is blue-blazed. However, within parkland, other trails merge and diverge so that there may be paint blazes (or metal triangles) of more than one color. Property owners along the *CT* employ blue paint as a boundary marker. Painted *CT* blazes are two by six inch rectangles at roughly eye level and face the direction of travel.

Road Access
See entries for individual sections.

Maps
PATC Map 5/6 and USGS Maps: Harpers Ferry, WV; Middletown, MD.

Gambrill State Park Trail Guide is for sale at ranger station and from http://shopdnr.com/westernmarylandtrailguides.aspx

Cunningham Falls State Park: http://www.dnr.state.md.us/publiclands/pdfs/cunningham_map.pdf

Catoctin Mountain Park: www.nps.gov/cato click on "view park map"

Shelters, Campsites, and Other Public Facilities
Gambrill State Park offers camping near the trails southern terminus in the Rock Run Area (31 sites and several small, furnished cabins). Gambrill State Park hours are 8 a.m. to sunset April through October and 10 a.m. to sunset November through March. There is no overnight parking at the southern trailhead because of thefts that have occurred in this area.

Cunningham Falls State Park has two campgrounds, the Manor Area (31 campsites, mile 16 northbound) and William Houck Area (140 campsites, mile 21 northbound). The Maryland State Park Reservations toll free number is 1-888-432-CAMP/2267. The William Houck and Manor Areas are open April through October. The Houck Area has a pay phone at the check-in gate and camp store on its Addison Run Circle 0.5 miles uphill on the campground road from its junction with the *CT*.

Owens Creek Campground in Catoctin Mountain Park is located near the northern terminus. (301-663-9388) www.nps.gov/cato. Owens Creek is open mid-April to the third weekend in November.

Potable *water* is available at campgrounds during their open season. Picnic areas have *water* available during their active season.

Additional information about the trail and facilities is available by contacting Gambrill and Cunningham Falls State Park (301-271-7574) or Catoctin Mountain Park (301-663-9388).

Two PATC rental cabins are situated along the *CT*, with hike-in and one with drive-in access. The rich history and location of either cabin make them ideal base camps for enjoying the *CT* and vicinity. Olive Green Cabin (4 bunks, primitive log cabin) is reached from the *CT* at its northernmost intersection with Catoctin Hollow Rd by a 0.3 mile road walk towards Hunting Creek Lake. Catoctin Hollow Cabin is described in Section VI and will be available for rental in mid-2015. Cabin information and reservation instructions is posted at http://www.patc.net under the 'Cabins' link. Tent camping is not permitted around cabins.

In emergencies, contact Catoctin Mountain Park at 301-663-9343. Report safety hazards or illegal activities on public lands to Park Watch at 1-800-825-7275 or a park employee. The *CT* occasionally crosses and borders private property where activities prohibited on park land (such as target shooting, motocross, ATV riding) are lawfully pursued.

Supplies

Potable water is not readily available along the *CT*. Campgrounds and picnic areas are sources during their active season. The southernmost 16 miles of *CT* has no trailside potable water sources. Carry adequate water for the season, exertion level and duration of your hike. With proper use of portable purification devices, the plentiful streams and springs can serve as water sources.

The *CT* terrain and footing varies from easy (Hamburg Rd to Delauter Rd) to challenging (Bobs Hill, Clifford Hollow). Any hike over 5 miles is almost sure to encounter grades steeper than ten percent, rutted tread, unavoidable pointed rocks and loose stone.

An added note on emergency equipment. Do not rely on mobile phone service to cope with emergencies. Signal strength varies by network and distance from populated areas. Despite antenna arrays along the trail, the mountainous terrain creates service shadows that extend for miles. Bring and rely on a first aid kit, know how to use it, and carry a quality map to indicate routes for assistance.

Olive Green Cabin   PATC

CT Section I.
Gambrill State Park Road to Hamburg Road
5.8 mi

NOTE: Southern end of *CT* initially is blazed with blue, black and red blazes.

Road Access

Southern end of section at Gambrill State Park Rd:
From US 40 west of Frederick, turn at sign for Gambrill State Park, located two miles outside of Frederick city limits. From the Hagerstown side, take US 40 eastbound and bear left on Shookstown Road for 0.5 mile. Follow Gambrill Park Road uphill, ignoring left forks. At 0.8 mi uphill from the junction with Shookstown Road, turn right at the gated trailhead parking lot (NAD83 N39° 27.733', W77° 29.478'). There are 20 spaces. Cars may be left overnight if the owner notifies the ranger on duty or calls the park headquarters at 301-271-7574.

Northern end of section at Hamburg Rd:
See *CT* Section II.

SECTION HIGHLIGHTS

Gambrill State Park – Named for prominent Frederick County conservationist, James H. Gambrill, this park entered the state park system in 1937 as a gift from Frederick County to the City of Frederick and to Maryland state. Its stonework and original structures were constructed by the Civilian Conservation Corps during the Great Depression. The Rock Run Area offers picnicking, camping and a small fishing lake at the lower, southernmost end of the park. The High Knob Area offers scenic views to the east, south, and west from the Tea Room at its 1600-foot summit and from three stone overlooks along the parks 16 miles of trails.

N-S	TRAIL DESCRIPTION	

0.0	**Gambrill State Park** Trailhead parking lot. Blue-blazed *CT* adjoins east side of lot between smaller of two roofed kiosks and paved road. A large model of parks trail system is in larger kiosk. Black and red trails coincide with *CT*.	5.8
0.2	Northbound: Stay west where red-blazed trail branches east. Southbound: Red-blazed trail joins. Proceed straight.	5.6
0.8	Junction of green-blazed trail that follows an old logging road. Northbound: Turn east onto old logging road, following blue, black and green blazes. Shortly ahead, turn west, uphill, leaving road, climbing eastern flank of ridge. Southbound: Fork away from green trail, on level blue- and black-blazed trail which shortly starts climbing.	5.0
1.2	Cross powerline cut.	4.6
1.3	Junction of black-blazed and green-blazed trails (heading uphill toward west) and unmarked road (heading downhill to east). Continue straight ahead. *Bootjack Spring* is 0.2 mi up green trail (reliable year-round, requires purification). Black trail switchbacks a mile up to North Frederick Overlook and daytime parking along Gambrill Park Rd.	4.5
1.5	Junction with yellow-blazed trail. Northbound: Bear east (right), and follow blue and yellow blazes. Southbound: Fork away from yellow trail following blue blazes downhill.	4.3

SECTION HIGHLIGHTS

Hunting – The watershed and private land within and bordering parkland are popular with hunters. Some areas in parks also allow hunting. For hunting season details check www.dnr.state.md.us/ huntersguide. Hunting season is traditionally mid-September through January and mid-April through late May.

White Rocks Overlook   Rick Canter

TRAIL DESCRIPTION

1.7   Junction with dirt road, now a mountain bike trail. (Yellow-blazed trail goes west with access to Gambrill Park Rd 0.3 mi to west. No parking.) Northbound: Turn east on road for 0.1 mi. Southbound: Leave road west (left) at double blaze, following yellow and blue blazes.   **4.1**

1.8   Junction with dirt road. Northbound: Leave woods road west (left) at double blaze. Southbound: Turn east (right) onto road for 0.1 mi.   **4.0**

2.3   Stream near head of South Fork of Clifford Branch. The 2.5 mi in and out of Clifford Hollow are especially scenic. Some of hollow is privately owned. Northbound: Start a mile of descent along stream, crossing it five times. Trail enters property where **hunting** is common. Southbound: Cross stream final time and begin climb out of hollow. Remainder of *CT* is on no-hunting property.   **3.5**

3.1   Bottom of Clifford Hollow and main course of Clifford Branch. Woods roads enter on both banks from downhill side. When stepping stones are submerged, bushwhack up-stream to alternate crossings. Northbound: Cross stream then follow wide trail on north bank. Go 300 ft and make a hairpin westward turn, leaving stream and woods road that continues straight ahead. Watch blue blazes for eastward turn uphill at intersection with bike trails. Southbound: Steep descent into hollow bottoms out at intersection with multiple bike trails before reaching stream. Follow blue blazes, first turning west then rounding a hairpin east onto woods road for 300 ft. Cross Clifford Branch and proceed along its south fork, crossing it four more times in next mile.   **2.7**

SECTION HIGHLIGHTS

Dam – The island began as a massive beaver lodge that was abandoned, providing a foothold for vegetation.

Pond north of Gambrill State Park   Catherine Kelleher

| TRAIL DESCRIPTION |

3.6 Large, bright, milky quartz boulders line trail of upper slope toward northern side of Clifford Hollow. Tidy rock piles on more level sections of woods testify to a period when this land was farmed. **2.2**

4.0 Cross sunken old roadbed diagonally. Road is now a bike trail connecting to Gambrill Park Rd, 1.5 mi to west with parking for 5 vehicles. Private land boundaries in this area are marked with blue paint splashes resembling blazes. **1.8**

4.4 North end of very rocky, but nearly level, 0.1-mile stretch. **1.4**

4.6 Cross old woods road. **1.2**

4.7 Another trail, unblazed but well used, crosses diagonally. **1.1**

5.2 **Dam** forms a small pond. Northbound: Cross dam, join with and ascend on old woods road. Southbound: Leave road, walk dam, drop west from dam at double blaze. **0.6**

5.3 Grassy woods road enters from compass southwest. This is now a relatively level bike trail connecting to sunken old roadbed (noted above) and Gambrill Park Rd. **0.5**

5.5 Junction marked with blazed 4x4 post on inside of turn. Northbound: Cross intermittent streambed 100 yd before post. Leave wide path, turning west at post onto narrow trail. Southbound: Turn east at 4x4 post onto wider path and cross intermittent streambed in 100 yd. **0.3**

5.8 Hamburg Rd. (Gambrill Park Rd is 0.4 mi to west.) **0.0**

CT Section II.
Hamburg Road to Delauter Road
3.1 mi

Road Access

Southern end of section at Hamburg Rd:
Parking for 10 vehicles on southern side of Hamburg Rd may be reached from two directions: (GPS coordinates for parking lot: NAD83 N39° 30.949', W77° 29.465')

Access 1. From southern trailhead parking lot in Gambrill Park: Continue uphill to junction. Turn right on Gambrill Park Rd for 3.6 mi to crossroads. Gambrill Park Rd continues straight. Highland School Rd goes left; Hamburg Rd goes right and Catoctin Trail crosses 0.4 mi downhill from intersection.

Access 2. From Frederick: On Rosemont Ave/Yellow Springs Rd. In Yellow Springs, at intersection with Bethel Rd, a four-way stop, Rosemont becomes Hamburg Rd. Continue on it for 5.5 mi to crossing of Catoctin Trail. Hamburg Rd changes from pavement to gravel before its winding ascent up Catoctin Mt.

Northern end of section at Delauter Rd:
See *CT* Section III.

Alternate access on Fishing Creek Rd: To reach mile point 2.1 northbound/1.1 southbound via a 0.3-mile connector trail from parking area on uphill side of Fishing Creek Rd. (See Section IV, Access 2 for access via Mountaindale Rd.) Take left fork just west of Fishing Creek Reservoir. In 1.2 mi turn left on Fishing Creek Rd. Proceed 0.5 mi to a parking space on right for approximately four cars. Hike uphill through gate on a woods road approximately 0.3 mi to meet *CT*. Turn right if going north on trail; left if going south.

N-S	TRAIL DESCRIPTION	

0.0 Hamburg Rd. Northbound: Cross road at east (downhill) end of parking area and enter woods at blue blaze. Continuing on from Section I, bear diagonally east. *Warning*: It is easy to mistakenly take more conspicuous, unblazed trail straight across the road. Southbound: Cross road to parking area. **3.1**

1.1 Skirt two ponds along their eastern banks. Trail is joined and crossed by service roads and fishing paths leading around and away from ponds. Carefully follow blue blazes. **2.1**

1.4 Branch of Fishing Creek. Northbound: Bear west after passing mining depression in hill to east and just before crossing intermittent stream. Then, curve east. Southbound: Bear west approaching intermittent stream, cross and curve east. Pass west of mine pit. **1.7**

1.6 Fishing Creek. Northbound: Turn east just before crossing. Southbound: Cross streambed and curve west. **1.5**

2.0 Junction of trail and road leading 0.3 mi to alternative access on Fishing Creek Rd (see access information above). A 6x6 signpost marks inside corner of sharp turn. **1.1**

2.7 Northbound: Turn east, downhill, on old woods road, shortly passing two old woods roads leading east. Continue straight on road, which is public right-of-way, passing through private property. Pass house and shed on east. Stay on gravel road. Southbound: Bear west, leaving woods as it goes straight. **0.5**

SECTION HIGHLIGHTS

Charcoal hearths – These terraced circles, 30 feet in diameter, appear throughout what are now backwoods areas and mark where colliers practiced their craft of making charcoal for the iron industry. The hearth holds a mound of compactly stacked hardwood covered with a layer of dirt to restrict oxygen. As a hearth smoldered for several days and nights, the collier would skillfully regulate the entry of air, to produce charcoal instead of worthless ashes. Forests surrounding iron furnaces were often clearcut to fuel the young nations hunger for iron. The *CT* passes beside or crosses over approximately 10 charcoal hearths between here and Rt 77.

Blazed path on the trail   Darrell Midgette

	TRAIL DESCRIPTION	

2.8 Trail crosses a **charcoal hearth** 25 feet south of a round brass survey marker tagged "PL573," mounted on a post.   **0.3**

3.1 Delauter Rd. Southbound: Walk gravel driveway, a public right-of-way through private property. Pass house and shed on west. Proceed uphill, passing woods roads joining from downhill side.   **0.0**

CT Section III.
Delauter Road to Steep Creek Road
2.6 mi

Road Access

Southern end of section at Delauter Rd:

Access 1. From junction of Gambrill Park Rd and Hamburg Rd: Continue 2.6 mi on Gambrill Park Rd to Delauter Rd. Here two third-class roads come from left; Gambrill Park Rd continues straight. Delauter Rd is on right. Turn right for 0.6 mi to crossing of Catoctin Trail. No parking lot exists, but uphill of the trail crossing are a few spots where the shoulder is wide and firm.

Access 2. Follow directions in Section IV, Access 2, for reaching Mountaindale Rd. One mile beyond Fishing Creek Reservoir, turn left onto Delauter Rd and go 0.8 mi, crossing ford, to intersection with Catoctin Trail. Except during dry conditions, ford depth is 10-12 inches and best negotiated with a vehicle having a high wheelbase.

Northern end of section at Steep Creek Rd:
See *CT* Section IV.

N-S	TRAIL DESCRIPTION	
0.0	Delauter Rd. Northbound: Cross road diagonally downhill and enter woods at blue blaze. Southbound: Cross road diagonally uphill and turn onto gravel driveway.	2.6
0.3	Pond to compass west. Pass by on dam.	2.3
0.8	Road enters from left (west). Turn right; blaze on post.	1.8
1.9	Turn left on forest road. Sign on tree indicates trail relocation.	0.7
2.5	Steep Creek. May be difficult to cross after rain.	0.1
2.6	Junction, 80 ft from Steep Creek Rd. Northbound: Turn east (right) at intersection and reach Steep Creek Road. Southbound: After descending from shoulder, turn west (left) continuing downhill.	0.0

CT Section IV.
Steep Creek Road to Gambrill Park Road
2.2 mi

Road Access

Southern end of section at Steep Creek Rd (labeled Fishing Creek Rd on some maps):

Access 1. From junction of Gambrill Park Rd and Delauter Rd, continue 2.7 mi as Gambrill Park Rd changes to gravel, reaching Steep Creek Rd (a/k/a Fishing Creek Rd) and turn sharply right. On Steep Creek Rd, the Catoctin Trail crossing is 0.8 mi downhill. Parking on wide shoulder for 4-6 vehicles. Avoid blocking access to gated fire road.

Access 2. From Frederick, go north 11 mi, on US 15 turn left at the Stull Rd exit. Follow Stull Rd 0.5 mi to Mountaindale Rd and turn right. In 1.5 mi., to stay on Mountaindale, make sharp left immediately after crossing creek. In another 0.7 mi. reach edge of the Fishing Creek Watershed (formerly Frederick Municipal Watershed) where road becomes gravel. Continue uphill on gravel road. At 0.4 mi., just beyond Fishing Creek Reservoir, road divides. Take left fork. In about 3.1 mi Delauter Rd enters from left. At this junction the name Mountaindale Rd changes to Steep Creek Rd. Continue ahead for 1.4 mi to trail crossing.

Northern end of section at Gambrill Park Rd:
See *CT* Section V.

N-S	TRAIL DESCRIPTION	
0.0	Steep Creek Rd. Northbound: Cross diagonally east to gated fire road/trail. Southbound: Cross road diagonally to west.	2.2
0.5	"Turnpike" trail over formerly flooded area.	1.7
0.7	Junction with woods road. A signpost on inside corner of turn.	1.5
1.4	Side road (blocked) leads compass east to pond. Inlet to north of side road is sometimes flooded. Trail skirts side of pond.	0.8
1.8	Trail passes pond on west; trail is on top of earthen dam. (Pond is on one of headwaters of Little Fishing Creek.)	0.4
1.9	Road from pond joins northbound trail from the west, along hillside. Southbound: Bear west. High density and uniform age of trees here marks an area clearcut following severe gypsy moth damage.	0.3
2.2	Gambrill Park Rd.	0.0

CT Section V.
Gambrill Park Road to Catoctin Hollow Road
2.0 mi

NOTE: Some trails in Cunningham Falls State Park are marked with colored metal triangles rather than paint blazes.

Road Access
Southern end of section at Gambrill Park Rd:

Access 1. From junction of Gambrill Park Rd and Steep Creek Rd, continue 2.3 mi on Gambrill Park Rd to Catoctin Trail crossing parking area on right side for six vehicles. Do not block access to gated fire road.

Access 2. Follow directions in Section IV, Access 2 for reaching Mountaindale Rd and Fishing Creek Reservoir. Just beyond Fishing Creek Reservoir, road divides. Take right fork (Gambrill Park Rd) 3.1 mi to Catoctin Trail crossing. Parking area on left side of road (this lot is prone to overnight vandalism).

Northern end of section at Catoctin Hollow Rd:
See *CT* Section VI.

View from Cat Rock

Catherine Kelleher

SECTION HIGHLIGHTS

Cunningham Falls State Park – Named for one of its feature attractions, a 78-foot waterfall on Big Hunting Creek. It is Maryland's longest cascading waterfall. The park was formed in 1936 to demonstrate how overexploited, marginal land could be restored. Depression era efforts of the Works Progress Administration and Civilian Conservation Corps laid the groundwork for the facilities now in place. In 1954, control of the land south of Rt 77 was returned to the State of Maryland for this park. Other popular attractions are Hunting Creek Lake, Cat Rock, and the Maple Syrup Festival held annually in mid-March at the William Houck Area. Park has two campgrounds, the Manor Area (31 campsites, mile 16 northbound) and William Houck Area (140 campsites, mile 21 northbound), open April through October. For further details, see *"Shelters, Campgrounds and Other Public Facilities,"* above.

White Rocks Overlook – Provides fine view to east. This is sometimes called the Hatchery Overlook as the state fish hatcheries are visible directly below. The stretch just north of White Rocks is known as Machete Alley because of the dense undergrowth.

Charcoal hearth – The soil is unnaturally black on the crumbling lip of this hearth. Trailside hearths are common in this area because of the proximity to **Catoctin Furnace**.

N-S	TRAIL DESCRIPTION	

0.0	Gambrill Park Rd. DNR kiosk with Watershed hunting information in parking area. This lot floods and is prone to overnight vandalism. Northbound: Cross gravel road and enter at gate. Southbound: Cross gravel to gate on north side of parking area.	2.0
0.1	Trail intersection in clearing. Catoctin Trail goes straight ahead. Hunting information is posted at this, the boundary between Fishing Creek Watershed (south) and **Cunningham Falls State Park** (north).	1.9
0.2	Pass social trails to **White Rocks Overlook**, 30 ft to compass east. Northbound: Start steep descent into Catoctin Hollow. Southbound, curve west.	1.8
0.3	Small gully. Northbound: 60 ft to charcoal hearth. Turn east, downhill. Southbound: Bear west, uphill.	1.7
0.6	Trail junction. Northbound: Bear west. Pass **Charcoal hearth**. Southbound: Follow blazing as trail ascends.	1.4
0.7	Double blaze. Northbound: Go east and down a bank for short distance, then descend on a winding trail. Southbound: Trail broadens and bends west after ascending.	1.3
0.8	Junction with woods road. Northbound: Road enters from east; bear west to join it. Southbound: At double blaze leave road, travel up bank to east that winds uphill.	1.2
0.9	Double blaze. Northbound: Leave woods road over downhill edge, bearing east on narrow path. Southbound: Scramble up bank and turn west onto wide woods road.	1.1

SECTION HIGHLIGHTS

Catoctin Furnace – Built nearby in 1778. This location offered several key resources needed for producing iron: hardwood forests for charcoal, iron ore, limestone as a catalyst and the water power of Little Hunting Creek to run air bellows. These ingredients combined here to supply cannonballs for the Continental Army and iron for local blacksmiths' forges to produce everyday implements for the growing local population. The furnace fires ultimately consumed the nearby forests and charcoal producers ranged farther away. Eventually, iron making here dwindled and moved on to other locations. Today, interpretive signs on the **Catoctin Furnace Trail** tell the story of this era at the one furnace tower (of three) that has been reconstructed. It can be reached by the Catoctin Furnace Trail.

Catoctin Furnace Trail – Spur trail near 6.5./0.2 leading from the *CT* east 0.4 mile through the **Manor Area** of Cunningham Falls State Park. See Section VI, Access 3 for access. **Catoctin Cottage**, reached by taking the Catoctin Furnace Trail 0.3 mile from the Manor Area Picnic Area to the furnace, then 0.1 south on Rt 806/Catoctin Furnace Road. The cottage once served the village of craftsman and laborers that sprung up around the furnace. The stone portion is over 200 years old. See "*Shelters, Campsites, and Other Public Facilities*" for access and rental information.

Earthen culverts – These are supported by fine nineteenth-century stonework, which is observable from the trail in one or two places.

N-S	TRAIL DESCRIPTION	
1.3	Trail skirts downhill edge of **charcoal hearth**. The soil is unnaturally black on the crumbling lip of this hearth. Trailside hearths are common in this area because of the proximity to **Catoctin Furnace**.	**0.7**
1.5	Trail crosses area (0.4 mi) of small gullies on **earthen culverts**. Damage from Superstorm Sandy is evident. Stay alert to blazes.	**1.5**
1.9	Trail passes near house.	**0.1**
2.0	Catoctin Hollow Rd. (US 15 is 0.3 mi east.) Northbound: Double blaze with paved road visible ahead; go left onto narrow trail, 200 ft to road. Southbound: Be especially attentive to blazing. Trail is sometimes narrower option at many intersections with woods roads.	**0.0**

CT Section VI.
Catoctin Hollow Road to
Route 77 (Foxville Road)
8.1 mi

Road Access

Southern end of section at Catoctin Hollow Road (first of two crossings):
From Frederick, take Route 15 north. At 1 mi after the exit for Rt 806 (Catoctin Furnace Rd), an extra left lane serves Cunningham Falls Sate Parks Manor Area and Catoctin Hollow Rd. Then follow directions below.

Access 1. Make a U turn from the median. On Rt 15 south, approximately 150 yards past the pedestrian overpass, turn right onto Catoctin Hollow Rd. Catoctin Trail crosses 0.3 mi from the Rt 15 intersection. Catoctin Hollow Rd. is narrow, rarely has a usable shoulder, and several apparent parking spots are posted no trespassing. See Access 2 and Access 3 below for parking.

Access 2. For parking at the southern end. From the median of Rt 15, cross the southbound lane into the Manor Area. Turn left after the gate house (this is a fee area in-season when staffed) to reach the picnic area and Visitor Center. Reach the *CT* at the downhill end of the lot (about 50 spaces), using paths that link picnic tables along Little Hunting Creek. Follow riparian path upstream 0.1 mi to where blue blazes are encountered. Modern restrooms and water fountain (seasonal operation, usually May-Sept.) at the lower end of the parking area. (GPS coordinates for parking lot: NAD83 N39° 35.332', W77° 26.137')

Access 3. For parking at Southern end. To start a *CT* hike at Catoctin Furnace (0.4 mi from *CT*), bear right off Rt 15 at the exit for Rt 806 (Catoctin Furnace Rd). Travel 0.8 mi on Rt 806 to the signed, paved parking area (approximately 15 spaces) for Catoctin Furnace on the left.

Interpretive exhibits at the furnace explain its operation and history. The Catoctin Furnace Trail to the north of the parking lot connects to the Manor Area Picnic Area (see Access 2 above) via the Rt 15 pedestrian footbridge. Signs along the trail tell of the iron industry and ruins of structures that supported the furnace.

Alternate Access at middle of section at Catoctin Hollow Road (second of two crossings):
Section VI crosses Catoctin Hollow Rd at 4.8 northbound, 1.9 southbound.

Access 1. Follow directions in Section VI, Access 1 for reaching Catoctin Hollow Rd first crossing. Continue on Catoctin Hollow Rd approximately 5 mi to trail crossing. Parking (3 spaces) on the left 0.1 mi after *CT*.

Access 2. Follow directions in Section VII to reach Rt 77/Foxville Rd. At 0.1 mi after passing the Catoctin Mountain Park Visitor Center, turn left onto Catoctin Hollow Road leading to the William Houck Area. Go straight past the turn for Hunting Creek Lake at 1.3 mi. The *CT* crosses 0.4 mi farther. Parking at hunters lot 0.3 mi past William Houck Dr/Lake entrance.

Northern end of section at Md 77:
See *CT* Section VII.

Little Hunting Creek – When water is high, cross by using the highway bridge on Route 15. Southbound: Reach Rt 15 by passing through Manor Area Picnic Area, to east of Trail. Cross on Rt 15 bridge, then return to *CT* by following trail that parallels the creek or taking Catoctin Hollow Rd west to trail. Northbound: Return to Catoctin Hollow Rd and hike downhill to Rt 15 and hike against traffic on shoulder. Cross on highway bridge and enter Manor Area Picnic Area, to west of highway just after the bridge, then follow path west to intersection with *CT*.

Manor Area Picnic Area – Has ample parking and a **Visitor Center** with 200 nature and other exhibits. See *"Shelters, Campsites, and Other Public Facilities."* In summer, programs are conducted on wildlife and conservation themes. The picnic area offers approximately 8 first-come, first-served tables along the creek, a reserved-for-fee 30-table picnic pavilion, restrooms and *water* (in season). This is the trailhead for Bobs Hill Trail (yellow blazed).

Manor Area Campground – North of picnic area, provides seasonal camping with 31 drive-up spaces. See *"Shelters, Campsites, and Other Public Facilities."*

Bobs Hill Trail – Trail to Bobs Hill (view) begins at Manor Area Visitor Center (upper) parking lot, which services Manor Area Picnic Area and Manor Area Campground. Enter woods at sign opposite upper parking lot on north side of Visitors Center. Joins *CT* in 0.3 mi. For the lowest 0.3 mi, this trail offers a somewhat easier route than the *CT* (6.7/1.1) by going through Manor Picnic Area to upper parking area and the beginning of Bobs Hill Trail. This route, which uses yellow blazes and metal triangles, is also steep but generally easier underfoot.

N-S	TRAIL DESCRIPTION	

0.0 Catoctin Hollow Road. Pass through rusty gateway on north shoulder of road. Upper 0.2 mi switchbacks within bottom of a deep manmade trough. — **8.1**

0.2 Cross **Little Hunting Creek** on stones. (See high water directions below.) A fence and signage immediately upstream of crossing mark private property. Stay to east. Downstream 0.1 mi, **Catoctin Furnace Trail** adjoins picnic area, leading to **Catoctin Cottage**. Northbound: After crossing creek, turn downstream/away from property line. Look east for wooden deck across an intermittent swampy area. After deck, switchback uphill. Southbound: Descend steep sidehill to stream bank. After crossing short deck, turn east. Cross Hunting Creek below boundary signs and pickup *CT* on opposite bank. — **7.6**

0.6 Northbound: Turn left at junction. White-blazed trail to right goes to Manor Area Visitors Center. Southbound: Turn right at junction. White-blazed trail to left goes to Manor area Visitors Center. — **7.2**

1.1 Junction with **Bobs Hill Trail**. Downhill, Bobs Hill Trail leads 0.3 mi to **Manor Area Visitor Center.** Uphill, two trails are merged to Bobs Hill summit/overlooks. Bobs Hill Trail uses yellow blazes and metal triangles. *CT* uses traditional painted blue blazes. (For alternate route that may be easier underfoot, see **Bobs Hill Trail** description.) Northbound: Turn west at intersection and bear east uphill. Ascend steadily, at times steeply. Southbound: Turn east at blazed post onto narrower *CT*, unless opting for alternate route. — **6.7**

SECTION HIGHLIGHTS

Bobs Hill Overlooks – The overlook to the east offers a somewhat obstructed view from a long narrow ridge towards Thurmont. Straight down is an interesting talus slope showing the power of weather to slowly fracture the stone supporting the overlook and reshape the landscape. The overlook west of the *CT* has unobstructed views to south from rocky cliff. The side trail branches nearing the edge. The more accessible but narrower view is to the left. A rock scramble for the adventurous gains an excellent vantage offered down the right fork, upon an outcropping of Weverton Quartzite injected with veins of milky quartz.

Cat Rock Trail – 1.5 mi east to Cat Rock and to Hunting Creek Lakes dam via Old Misery Trail.

William Houck Area – Includes 44-acre Hunting Creek Lake with boating, swimming and picnicking, 140 drive-in campsites, a campstore, and trailhead for trails to Cunningham Falls. See "*Shelters, Campsites, and Other Public Facilities.*"

Olive Green Cabin – A small cabin (bunks for 4) in the PATC rental system, built in the German log cabin style. The cabin is locked. It does not offer water or restroom facilities. See "*Shelters, Campsites, and Other Public Facilities*" for access and rental information.

Hunting – DNR signage indicates this area is open for ADA hunting annually from Nov 26 to Dec 24.

N-S

TRAIL DESCRIPTION

1.8 From this point to several miles north, laurel grows profusely. Forest floor is littered with deadfall oaks, casualties of severe gypsy moth infestations in late 1980s.   **6.0**

2.8 **Bobs Hill Overlooks,** marked by conspicuous 6x6 inch post. West overlook is 400 ft on level trail. East overlook is 150 ft slightly uphill.   **5.0**

3.5 Signpost at junction with yellow-blazed **Cat Rock Trail.** Go straight. Northbound: Blue blazes no longer accompanied by yellow. Southbound: Blue and yellow metal blazes occur together as trails merge for the next 2.3 mi.   **4.3**

3.6 Highest elevation on Catoctin Trail, 1,770 ft.   **4.2**

3.7 *Caution*: Boulder field, difficult footing. Trail narrows, with understory dominated by blueberry bushes.   **4.1**

4.5 *CT* hops between woods roads. Stay alert to blazes and intersections blocked by clutter where trail leaves woods roads.   **3.3**

5.3 Switchback turn. Northbound: Turn sharply west and proceed through groves of towering tulip poplars. Southbound: Turn sharply east and continue climbing steeply for 0. 2 mi, after which slope moderates.   **2.5**

6.0 Cross blacktop Catoctin Hollow Rd. Entrance road to **William Houck Area** of Cunningham Falls State Park is 0.3 mi north. **Olive Green Cabin** is reached by a short road walk towards lake. A small hunters parking area is roadside 0.1 mi east. **Hunting** is allowed in this area of park.   **1.8**

S-N

Catoctin Hollow Cabin – A modern PATC cabin that sleeps 8. Access by spur trail. Cabin should be available for rental by July 2015.

Cunningham Falls Cliff Trail – Descends to base of Cunningham Falls. This is a pleasant, though sometimes crowded (summer weekends), side excursion to the 78-ft cascade.

Campground Trail – Ascends gently to Addison Run loop of Houck Area campground. Distances are about 0.3 mi to pavement, 0.7 mi to camp store. *Water* is available at campground loop restroom during camping season.

Dead hemlock trees – This forest is in transition from tall, shade-casting hemlock (an evergreen) to birches and maples that also favor the hollows moist, loamy soil. The hemlocks succumbed in the 1990s to an infestation by the woolly adelgid. The tiny insects so weakened their stately hosts that few hemlocks survive today in the hollows they once dominated.

Descending Bobs Hill   Catherine Kelleher

N-S   TRAIL DESCRIPTION

6.1   Cross stream. (If high water makes stream impassable, use campground road (on north side) and Catoctin Hollow Rd (on south side) to go east to Cunningham Falls State Park entrance and then return west to trail, to avoid stream crossing.)   **1.7**

6.2   Cross intermittent stream bed. When wet, better crossing opportunities are upstream.   **1.6**

6.3   Northbound: Uphill trail (sharp left) that leads 0.3 mi to PATC's **Catoctin Hollow Cabin** (rental). Cabin has modern amenities and sleeps 8. Southbound: Spur trail on right that leads to cabin. Continue straight on Catoctin Trail downhill toward stream.   **1.5**

6.5   Cross powerline.   **1.3**

6.8   Paved road at **William Houck Area Campground** check-in station. In season, potable *water* is available at either spigot serving RV cleanouts. (To east, road continues to Catoctin Hollow Rd.) Northbound: Cross blacktop and up embankment at *CT* trail sign. Southbound: Enter woods across parking lanes and RV cleanout stations.   **0.9**

7.1   Junction of yellow-blazed **Cunningham Falls Cliff Trail** which merges for a short distance with *CT* northbound. Southbound: Bear east at 6x6 post onto less-traveled *CT*. Proceeding straight on yellow trail leads to Falls trailhead 0.5 mi.   **0.7**

7.3   Junction of *CT* and **Cunningham Falls Cliff Trail** and **Campground Trail** (orange). Northbound: Bear west at post to continue on *CT*. Southbound: Yellow trail merges onto *CT*. Both yellow and blue blazes mark trail next 0.2 mi.   **0.5**

SECTION HIGHLIGHTS

Catoctin Mountain Park and **Visitor Center** – Although 'National' is absent from its name, this is a National Park. The park started from a 1936 federal initiative by the Works Progress Administration and Civilian Conservation Corps to research and demonstrate progressive conservation practices. Subsistence farming had become increasingly difficult after the loss of the American chestnut trees and soil depletion from generations of heavy use. The land was reforested and the park infrastructure developed by the CCC and WPA laborers following a government buyout and resettlement program.

Visitor Center – This is an excellent place to learn more of the natural and human history of the region. It is on Park Central Rd at MD 77, 1.7 mi east of the Catoctin Trail It is open year-round. It offers ample parking, *water*, restrooms, exhibits, a bookstore, and serves as a trailhead for the Blue Blazes Still trail, and for reaching the Charcoal Trail, Chimney Rock, Wolf Rock, Hog Rock and Thurmont Vista. Much of the paneling inside the Center came from blighted American chestnut trees, dead but still standing when the building was constructed.

Rt 77 is a narrow, dangerous road. You should enjoy your tour of the Visitor Center by driving there before or after your hike.

TRAIL DESCRIPTION

7.4   Promontory with overlook. Trail traverses rocky   **0.4**
face on north side. Note many large **dead hemlock
trees**. On rise 100 yd ahead is a very large black oak,
probably untouched for charcoal or lumber because
it grew in the yard of an early settler cabin.

7.5   The *CT* is on and off of woods roads that   **0.3**
honeycomb this prime bottomland, actively farmed
into the 1930s. Stay alert to blazes and intersections
purposefully blocked by clutter. Take note of the
masterfully laid dry stone walls.

7.8   Route 77 (Foxville Rd). Road is boundary between   **0.0**
Cunningham Fall State Park (to south) and **Catoctin
Mountain Park** (to north). **Visitor Center** is 1.7 mi
east on Rt 77. (*Do not hike the road.*) Northbound:
Bear west at double blaze. Turn east on far side
of waist-high boulder and descend to Md 77. To
continue hike, turn east on Md 77, cross culvert over
Hunting Creek and enter woods at gate on other
side of bridge. Southbound: From fire road gate,
cross road below bridge, cross Big Hunting Creek
on road culvert. Proceed 100 ft and turn west from
road up a short hill beside a rock face. Turn west at
top of rise.

CT Section VII.
Md 77 to Mt. Zion Road
4.9 mi

NOTE: CT follows horse trails through Catoctin Mountain and is on, or parallel to, Manahan Rd for more than a mile. Horse trail blazes are on posts and are marked with a horseshoe.

Road Access

Southern end of section at Md 77: From US 15 near Thurmont take Md 77 west. Pass Catoctin Park Visitor Center in 2.9 mi. In another 1.7 mi reach bridge over Hunting Creek where the *CT* crosses Rt 77. The narrow shoulders on Rt 77 do not support parking here. The gated fire road pull-off must not be blocked. This crossing can offer hikers a place for a momentary drop-off or pick-up, but is not suited to longer duration parking.

Alternate access at middle of section at Park Central Rd: Section VII crosses Park Central Rd at 1.1 mi northbound/3.1 mi southbound, near the Chestnut Picnic Area.

Access 1. Follow directions above to the Visitor Center and turn right on Park Central Rd. Follow for approximately 5.5 mi and park at Chestnut Picnic Area. A connector trail leads west to the *CT* from the road entrance to the picnic area. Park Central Road may be closed at the Park's discretion.

Access 2. A quicker, less scenic route to Chestnut Picnic Area is to pass the *CT* crossing at Hunting Creek, and turn right after 1.5 mi onto Foxville-Deerfield Rd, then right again onto Manahan after 0.3 mi. Proceed 1 mi to intersection with Park Central Rd, then right 0.5 mi on it to the picnic area.

Alternate access at middle of section at Owens Creek Campground on Foxville-Deerfield Rd

Section VII crosses the entrance to Owens Creek Campground at 2.4 mi northbound/1.8mi southbound. Follow directions above to Foxville-Deerfield Rd, but proceed straight at the fork with Manahan Rd. At 0.7 mi after fork, bear right and follow signage to Owens Creek Campground. The *CT* crosses Owens Creek on the car bridge at the campground entrance. Parking in loop spaces at the campground is for campers. There is an overflow/hikers parking lot 0.1 mi on the right before the campground entrance.

Northern end of section at Mt Zion Rd:
See *CT* Section VIII.

SECTION HIGHLIGHTS

Camp Greentop – Noted for its many picturesque log cabins, built of native American chestnut in 1937 by the Works Progress Administration (WPA). The cabins were specifically constructed to meet the needs of its first tenants, the Baltimore League for Crippled Children. It was among the first outdoor facilities specifically designed for handicapped campers, has been in constant use by many special needs groups (except for wartime occupation during World War II) and is listed on the National Registry of Historic Places. Organized groups of 60 or more can rent the camp for weeks or weekends from April through mid-June and mid-August until October 31st. The Dining Hall and Recreation Hall are available for conferences year-round. The cabins can sleep 129 people. There is a sports field and swimming pool available in-season for week-long groups.

Chestnut Picnic Area – Offers parking, approximately 20 first-come, first-served tables and restroom facilities. A 0.1 mi connector trail on the north side of the road links the *CT* and picnic area. This trail continues eastward to the gentle Spicebush loop trail (0.2 mi) with a spur leading to the back end of the picnic area.

Catoctin Mountain Park Visitor Center – See Section VI highlights.

N-S	TRAIL DESCRIPTION	
0.0	Rt 77. Northbound: From north side of road, follow blue blazes along gated fire road on east side of Hunting Creek. As creek veers off to west, continue straight ahead on fire road.	**4.9**
0.2	Intermittent springs on uphill side of trail.	**4.7**
0.3	Pass large stone wall running perpendicular to trail on uphill side.	**4.6**
1.1	Fire road and path meet. Buildings to east uphill are **Camp Greentop**. Northbound: Leave fire road east onto path. Traverse swath of forest decimated by a tornado in September, 2004. Southbound: Turn west onto fire road.	**3.8**
1.2	Water well cap in middle of trail. Cross service road for the nearby pumphouse. Water is not available to hikers.	**3.7**
1.4	Woods road meets footpath. Mound of earth with inverted J-pipes covers an underground water tank.	**3.5**
1.6	Cross Park Central Rd. To compass east 0.1 mi is **Chestnut Picnic Area**, beyond which the road twists to **Catoctin Mountain Park Visitor Center**. To west is Manahan Rd. Portions of both roads are closed in winter. Trail parallels park road on north side before diverging.	**3.3**
1.8	Junction Manahan Rd. Northbound: Turn east along road for 0.1 mi. Southbound: Leave Manahan Rd by turning west into woods at double blaze.	**3.1**

SECTION HIGHLIGHTS

Owens Creek Campground – Provides seasonal camping for modest-sized tents and trailers/RVs on a first-come, first-served basis. See *"Shelters, Campsites, and Other Public Facilities."* On summer weekends, arriving early on Friday afternoon may help secure a campsite. Restrooms are a *water* source for hikers during camping season.

Stream in Manor Area   Catherine Kelleher

N-S	TRAIL DESCRIPTION	

1.9 Junction Manahan Rd. Northbound: Turn west behind metal gate then *immediately* turn east onto narrow trail that parallels Manahan Rd, passing a sign for horse trail. Southbound: At metal gate begin 0.1 mi road walk. **3.0**

2.6 Gravel road. Northbound: Turn east on gravel road for 60 ft then turn west onto trail, crossing a drainage channel. Do not return to Manahan Rd through metal bar gate. Southbound: Cross stream at roadside culvert and parallel Manahan Rd. At gravel side road, turn east for 60 ft then turn east onto trail. **2.3**

2.9 Cross stream flowing from culvert under Manahan Rd. Trail parallels Manahan Rd. **2.0**

3.2 Cross Foxville-Deerfield Rd at sign for **Owens Creek Campground**. Northbound: Turn west at sign marking entrance for campground. Cross bridge over Owens Creek and in about 125 ft turn east into woods. Southbound: Descend to Owens Creek at campground entrance. Turn west at road, walk 125 ft, cross bridge and turn east. Enter woods at 4x4 post on opposite side of road. **1.7**

3.7 Trail crosses through gap in stone walls that lace this area. **1.2**

4.0 Top of hill. Elevation approximately 1600 ft. **0.9**

4.2 Junction with woods road, now used as horse trail. Stay straight at wooden sign. A masterfully crafted and well-preserved dry stone wall parallels *CT* for a short distance. **0.7**

SECTION HIGHLIGHTS

Deerfield Nature Loop Trail – Departs the campground loop road at campsite #30, where an interpretive guide to its points of interest is available. Using a horse trail from its westernmost point, it offers an alternative to the *CT* with a milder ascent of the summit that the *CT* crosses north of Owens Creek Campground, or a 3 mi circuit returning on the *CT*.

Eroded stone foundation is trailside at this sign. Spicebush is abundant in this region, as are signs of an active agricultural community in the early 1900s. An old adage suggests that plentiful spicebush signifies rich soil for farming.

Alien spores lying in wait for unsuspecting hikers   Catherine Kelleher

N-S	TRAIL DESCRIPTION	

4.4 A branch of horse trail enters from west at wooden sign. Stay straight. Horse trail connects to **Deerfield Nature Loop Trail. Eroded stone foundation**. **0.5**

4.8 Woods road on edge of a field, and wide stone wall paralleling trail in woods. Northbound: Turn west upon reaching field. Southbound: Turn east into woods at horseshoe-imprinted 4x4 post. *It is easy to miss this turn.* **0.1**

4.9 Mt. Zion Rd and parking area. This is present northern terminus of Catoctin Trail. Mt. Zion Church and cemetery are on west side of road. **0.0**

CT Section VIII.
Mt. Zion Church to Appalachian Trail
2.1 miles

Road Access

Northern end of section at Mt Zion Rd:
From US 15 near Thurmont, go west on Md 77. Pass Cunningham Falls handicap parking lot to the crossroads with Stottlemeyer Rd on south (left) and Foxville-Deerfield Rd on north (right). Continue west, then turn north (right) onto Quirauk Church Rd, which becomes Mt. Zion Rd at Mt. Zion Church. The parking lot for Catoctin Mountain Park is on east beyond churchyard. (GPS coordinates for parking area: NAD83 N39° 40.323', W77° 29.907').

Across from trailhead   Catherine Kelleher

| TRAIL DESCRIPTION |

0.0 Mt. Zion Rd. Northbound: Cross road and follow it downhill compass south. Pass churchyard in 100 ft then fork away from Quirauk School Rd on Mt Zion Rd. Southbound: At Mt Zion Church, proceed straight as Quirauk School Rd merges with Mt Zion Rd. Proceed compass north 100 ft to junction with trail and parking area, just beyond Mt Zion Church and cemetery. **2.1**

0.6 Intersection of Raven Rock Rd (Rt 491) and Mt Zion Rd. Northbound: Merge onto wider road heading compass southwest and follow Raven Rock Rd/Rt 491. Southbound: Split away from larger road onto narrower Mt Zion Rd heading compass northeast. **1.5**

2.1 Intersection of Raven Rock Rd/Rt 491 and the Appalachian Trail. White blazes mark the *AT* at road crossing approximately 0.3 mi west from Ritchie Rd junction. Northbound Appalachian Trail: Enter woods at white blaze on north side of road. and climb steeply. Raven Rock Shelter is 1.0 mi north. Southbound Appalachian Trail: Trail parallels road between guardrail and stream for 0.1 mi. Look for blaze painted on highway side of guardrail. **0.0**

View of Harpers Ferry from Maryland Heights   Larry Broadwell

SIDE TRAILS

VIRGINIA AND WEST VIRGINIA

LOUDOUN HEIGHTS TRAIL
Distance: 1.6 Miles

This blue-blazed trail is an "in and out" trail to Split Rock and offers superb views of Harpers Ferry.

Camping and fires are prohibited throughout Harpers Ferry National Historical Park.

Cross reference: Virginia Section 1.

SECTION HIGHLIGHTS

Harpers Ferry Hostel and other services may be reached via the Sandy Hook bridge. From the northern end of Loudoun Heights Trail, follow the right shoulder of US 340 across the bridge to Maryland, take the former access ramp down to Sandy Hook Road, cross the guardrail and go 0.2 miles left (uphill) on Sandy Hook Road to the hostel, which is on the river side of the road. Total distance from Loudoun Heights trailhead: 0.9 miles. At the hostel, get directions to other services nearby.

SECTION HIGHLIGHTS

Charcoal hearths in this area supplied fuel for the federal arsenal at Harpers Ferry (the target of John Brown's famous 1859 raid). Watch for large semi-circles of flattened ground, where charcoal makers heaped felled trees, covered them with earth, and kept the pile smoldering for days to drive moisture out of the wood.

Orange-blazed trail – This 0.6 mi.-long trail starts at a charcoal hearth on the *AT* on the west slope of the mountain, follows an old road, then turns uphill at the powerline, switchbacking up to the Loudoun Heights Trail.

Rock redoubts – These structures, dating from the Civil War, were infantry ddate from the Civil War. Both Union and Confederate forces occupied these heights at various times, and control of this area often meant control of Harpers Ferry, which changed hands repeatedly during the war. Confederate Gen. John G. Walker's artillery bombarded Harpers Ferry defenses from this area in September of 1862, helping Stonewall Jackson to take the town and capture 12,000 Union soldiers.

Junction with *AT* – Intersection with *AT* atop Loudoun Heights. Trail follows old route of *AT* along Loudoun Heights, descending to US 340. Trail then follows US 340, crosses Potomac River on Sandy Hook Bridge and connects to *AT* in village of Sandy Hook. Parking is available along US 340 in the vicinity of trail's departure from it.

N-S	TRAIL DESCRIPTION	

0.0   Path on west side of trail leads a short distance to Split Rock, an interesting rock formation with superb views of Harpers Ferry, Elk Ridge and the Potomac River gorge. Southbound: Ahead, steep ascents alternate with gentler sections as the trail moves up to ridgeline. Northbound: Reach Split Rock on left.   **1.6**

0.2   Pass large rock pillar on west side of trail.   **1.4**

0.5   Short side path goes west to good views from powerline clearing. Southbound: Moderate ascent continues. Northbound: Alternating steep and gentle descents ahead.   **1.1**

0.7   Short side path to west offers views of upper Harpers Ferry (cemetery, Cliff House hotel), Bolivar, and Potomac River from powerline cut. Southbound: Ascend gradually. Northbound: Moderate descent ahead.   **0.9**

1.0   Pass upper end of **orange-blazed trail** that goes down west slope 0.6 miles to connect with *AT* at the site of an 1800s **charcoal hearth**.   **0.6**

1.5   Southbound: Enter section where remains of **rock redoubts** can be seen, especially on west side of trail. Northbound: Enter section where remains of **rock redoubts** can be seen.   **0.1**

1.6   **Junction with *AT*** in Virginia Section 1. Northbound: From *AT*, which dips west and downhill, follow ridge straight ahead on blue-blazed trail. *Camping and fires are prohibited in HFNHP.* Southbound: Blue-blazed Loudoun Heights Trail ends. To take the *AT* south, follow white rectangular blazes straight ahead. To take the *AT* north into Harpers Ferry, turn west and go downhill.   **0.0**

S-N

RIDGE-TO-RIVER TRAIL
Distance: 2.5 miles

The Ridge to River Trail is a 2.5 mile trail that leaves the Appalachian Trail in the area of Sand Springs and drops down the west side of the Blue Ridge, ending at the Shenandoah River.

PLEASE NOTE: Nearly this entire trail is located on private land. The public has permission to use the blue-blazed trail. Stay on the trail. There is no road or hiking access to the trail at the river end as the public does not have permission to hike or drive on other portions of private land. The closest trailhead, with substantial parking, is at the *AT* crossing of Va 7 near Snickers Gap, Route 7. The parking lot is at the intersection of Va 7 and Va 679, with the entrance from Va 679. It is 3.2 miles to hike north on the *AT* to the intersection with the Ridge-to-River Trail.

E-W	TRAIL DESCRIPTION	
	Westbound (downhill, towards river): Eastbound (uphill, away from river):	
0.0	Junction of blue blazed trail and *AT* (It is a 3 mile hike south to Va 7). Trail passes Sand Spring (on north side of trail) 200 yd west of junction with *AT*.	**2.5**
0.1	Westbound: Bear left onto forest road, continuing downhill. A minor powerline runs along road. Eastbound: Bear slightly right off forest road into woods.	**2.4**
0.6	Forest road (private) on north side of trail. Continue straight.	**1.9**
0.8	Forest road (private) on north. Continue straight.	**1.7**
0.9	Westbound: Trail bears left off powerline road and enters an area of mature beech trees. Eastbound: Trail exits area of beech trees, bearing slightly right onto a forest road. A minor powerline runs along road.	**1.6**

W-E

E-W	TRAIL DESCRIPTION	

1.0	Old forest road. Westbound: Cross road, leaving area of beech trees. Ahead, trail passes close to Rocky Branch Stream in a wide turn to right. Eastbound: Cross road and enter area of mature beech trees.	**1.5**
1.1	Westbound: Trail has sharply defined turn to left. Ahead, trail enters pine forest. Eastbound: Trail leaves pine forest area, has sharply defined turn to right. Ahead, in a wide turn to left, trail passes close to Rocky Branch Stream.	**1.4**
1.3	Sequence of closely spaced features. Westbound: Trail passes a property line marker (on right), leaves pine forest turning right onto a heavily-used forest road; continues straight on this road as other forest roads merge in left and right, then turns left on a forest road, and in 40 yd passes a gate (usually locked). Eastbound: Trail passes a gate (usually locked), turns right onto another forest road and continues straight on this road (at a slight Y in road, stay to left), then turns left leaving road and entering a pine forest, and in 70 feet passes a property line marker (on left).	**1.2**
1.4	Y-intersection of roads. Westbound: Stay to left. Eastbound: Stay to right.	**1.1**
1.8	Another forest road. Westbound: Turn right onto road. Eastbound: Turn left onto road.	**0.7**
1.9	Westbound: Road starts a steep descent. Eastbound: Road levels off. Continue on forest road.	**0.6**
2.2	Westbound: Steep descent ends at floodplain. Eastbound: Continue to follow road, which turns right, starting steep ascent.	**0.3**
2.5	Forest road ends at bank of Shenandoah River. Eastbound: Leave through woods and in 200 ft turn left on forest road.	**0.0**

SKY MEADOWS STATE PARK TRAILS

The 1,862 acre Sky Meadows State Park offers convenient access to the *AT*, a campground (0.75 mi from the Visitor Center parking lot), and some short circuit hikes with extraordinary views from the Park's high meadows. The trails have excellent footing (but some rocky areas) and are also notable for an abundance of dogwood. This is an excellent place for viewing hawks, eagles, butterflies, and wild flowers.

The Park is open from 8:00 a.m. to dusk daily and has a small entrance fee per car. Beside the parking lot is a Visitor Center and the Mt. Bleak house, built about 1820 and once owned by Col. Mosby's rangers. In the yard are thriving Kentucky coffee trees, offshoots of the largest of its kind in the state: 83 feet high, 7.5 feet wide, and more than 150 years old when it died.

The campground has tent pads at several of the sites, fire pits, pit toilet, and a hand-pump well (water must be boiled or disinfected, however). *AT* thru hiker site is located just below hand-pump well and marked as such. The camping fee is $15 per site (payment instructions are located at site) with a limit of six persons per site. Reservations are recommended and can be made by calling Virginia State Parks Reservation Center at 800-933-7275. Campers must arrive before the Park closes at dusk. Camping and fires are prohibited elsewhere in the Park. *Special procedures apply if you wish to park overnight in the Visitor Center. Call above number for details.*

For information call 540-592-3556 or visit the Park's web page at http://www.decr.virginia.go/state_parks/sky.html.

Cross-reference: Virginia Section 4.

Access: From I-66, take exit 23, US 17, north toward Delaplane and Paris (not the US 17 Business exit); or from US 50, take US 17 south. Turn west onto Va 710, Edmonds Lane, the Park entrance road.

North Ridge Trail
Distance: 1.7 miles (*blue-blazed*)

From Visitor Center

0.0 From road at west end of parking lot, take graveled path to left of private driveway.

0.1 Turn left onto gravel road. Ahead, turn right off road and cross stile. (For Gap Run Trail remain on gravel road another 0.2 mi.) Continue on path. Red-blazed Piedmont Overlook Trail intersects on right. Ascend steeply on hillside meadow with outstanding eastward view.

0.3 Bench under hickory tree.

0.5 Cross opening in old stone wall and turn left. Level.

0.6 Go straight and cross stile. Ascend into open woods on dirt path. Ahead, Piedmont Overlook Trail intersects on right. A little farther on, pass intersection with Ambassador Whitehouse Trail, on right. Trail undulates ahead through red oak, hickory, and American basswood.

0.8 Descend steeply.

0.9 Bench. Gap Run Trail intersects on left. Go straight, cross creek just ahead on rock causeway, and ascend, very steeply at times.

1.4 South Ridge Trail intersects on left. Bear right.

1.7 Junction with *AT*, in Virginia Section 4.

From AT

0.0 Junction with *AT*, in Virginia Section 4. Descend, very steeply at times.

0.3 South Ridge Trail intersects on right. Bear left.

0.9 Cross creek on rock causeway and pass Gap Run Trail, which intersects on right. (*AT* hikers should turn right here to reach campground.) Bench. Ascend steeply ahead.

1.0 Trail undulates ahead. Pass some American basswood. Ahead, Ambassador Whitehouse Trail intersects on left.

1.1   Piedmont Overlook Trail intersects on left, just before stile. Go straight. Ahead, the trail becomes graveled.

1.3   Turn right and cross opening in old stone wall. Descend steeply on hillside meadow with outstanding eastward view.

1.4   Bench under hickory tree.

1.6   Piedmont Overlook Trail intersects on left. Go straight, cross stile, and turn left onto gravel road ahead.

1.7   Turn right off road, onto gravel walkway and shortly reach parking lot by Visitor Center.

Ambassador Whitehouse Trail
Distance: 1.1 miles (*light blue–blazed*)

The Ambassador Whitehouse Trail Connects the North Ridge Trail in Sky Meadows State Park to the Appalachian Trail in the National Park Service Ovoka Tract. The trail offers excellent views from open meadows and provides access to loop hikes involving the Appalachian Trail, Old Trail and North Ridge Trail.

From intersection with North Ridge Trail

0.0   Ambassador Whitehouse Trail ascends steeply through several switchbacks.

0.2   Cross gas pipe line right-of-way with limited eastward view then trail levels out and begins a more gentle ascent.

0.5   Enter field following mowed path and light blue-blazed posts.

0.7   Trail turns to left along fence line at the excellent Paris view point. Piedmont Environmental Council stone wall memorial visible on north site of fence. Trail bears left from fence and follows path through open meadow.

1.1   Ambassador Whitehouse Trail terminates at the intersection with Appalachian Trail. Continuing south 0.8 mile on the Appalachian Trail leads to a junction with North Ridge Trail. Continuing north 0.7 mile on Appalachian Trail leads to junction with Old Trail.

Old Trail
Distance: 1.9 miles (*purple-blazed*)

In 2005 a section of the Appalachian Trail (*AT*) was relocated onto the US Park Service's Ovoca Tract, adjacent to Virginia's Sky Meadows State Park. The replaced section of the *AT* was designated the Old Trail and blazed purple. The Old Trail adds to the network of trails associated with Sky Meadows State Park and is useful in arranging a circuit hike.

The northern end of the Old Trail can be accessed by hiking 1.1 miles south from US 50 on the AT or by hiking north 0.7 miles from the AT/Ambassador Whitehouse Trail junction. The southern end of the Old Trail can be accessed 0.1 mile north from the AT/North Ridge Trail junction. The junctions with the purple-blazed Old Trail are well signed.

North to South

0.0 The Old Trail begins at junction with *AT* (Section 4, 1.1/10.7 mi).

0.2 Trail follows a narrow corridor paralleling old roadbed to east.

0.6 Turn right onto old roadbed.

0.7 Turn left onto sunken roadbed.

0.3 Bear right and descend.

1.4 Turn left and ascend a couple long switchbacks.

1.7 Turn right onto roadbed and immediately cross gas pipeline right-of-way. Good westward view. Turn left into woods immediately after crossing right-of-way. Enter Sky Meadows State Park.

1.9 Old Trail ends at junction with *AT* (Section 4, 2.5/9.3 mi). Continue south on *AT* 0.1 mi to junction with North Ridge Trail. Continue north on *AT* 0.7 mi to junction with Ambassador Whitehouse Trail.

Gap Run Trail
Distance: 1.0 mile (*orange-blazed*)

From Lower End. From road at west end of Visitor Center parking lot, take graveled path to left of private driveway for 0.1 mi. to reach beginning of Trail description.

0.0   Continue past entrance to North Ridge Trail, entering from right. Road follows an undulating lane between cow pastures.

0.3   Turn right and cross stile. (Straight ahead, 0.2 mi farther down road, Snowden Interpretive Trail begins.) Ahead, South Ridge Trail intersects on left. Go straight and ascend through meadow.

0.5   Cross stile and enter woods ahead.

0.6   Cross stream. Picnic table on right and at each campsite. Privies on left just ahead. Well with non-potable water, which must be boiled or disinfected. Road becomes grassy ahead. Pass tent sites designated by numbered posts.

0.8   Cross creek on rock causeway and ascend steeply.

1.0   Upper junction with North Ridge Trail, at 0.9 mi from *AT*.

From Upper End

0.0   Upper junction with North Ridge Trail, at 0.9 mi from *AT*. Descend steeply.

0.3   Cross creek on rock causeway.

0.4   Pass tent sites designated by numbered posts, and pass well with non-potable water, which must be boiled or disinfected. Just ahead, privies on right and picnic table on left. Each campsite also has a picnic table.

0.5   Cross stream. Ahead, cross stile and descend through meadow.

0.7   South Ridge Trail intersects on right. Go straight.

0.8   Cross stile and turn left onto gravel road. Road forms an undulating lane between cow pastures. (Snowden Interpretive Trail begins 0.2 mi down the gravel road to the right.)

1.0   Lower junction with North Ridge Trail, 0.1 mi from Visitor Center.

Snowden Interpretive Trail
Distance: 1.1 miles (*silver-blazed*)

Counterclockwise Loop beginning 0.3 mi from Visitor Center parking lot. From road at west end of parking lot, take graveled path to left of private driveway for 0.1 mi. intersection with North Ridge Trail, entering from right. Continue on road, which follows an undulating lane between cow pastures.

0.0   Pass junction with Gap Run Trail, entering from right. Ahead, twelve markers on this trail explain the ecology of these woods. Ascend old road originally constructed in the 1820s. Go right at fork ahead.

0.1   Descend, then level.

0.2   Ascend, then level. Undulates ahead.

0.3   Cross two bridges ahead and ascend.

0.4   Field on right. Bench on left overlooking woods.

0.5   Descend.

0.8   Cross bridge over intermittent stream. Ascend ahead.

0.9   Descend.

1.0   Road parallels a field on right. Ascend generally.

1.1   End of loop.

South Ridge Trail
Distance: 1.6 miles (*yellow-blazed*)

From Lower End. Follow directions for Lower End of Gap Run Trail to reach intersection of Gap Run and South Ridge trails.

0.0   Junction with Gap Run Trail.

0.1   Enter woods. Ahead, go straight past intersecting path and immense hickory. Ascend very steeply.

0.2 Hillside meadow with outstanding view. There is short detour to a bench a short distance up hill straight ahead. Turn left and descend to stay on Trail. Ahead, pass path that intersects on left.

0.3 Pass ruins on left and bear right onto old road. Then pass Snowden Manor ruins on left. Stone chimney, house foundation, and well are visible. Next, turn right and skirt foot of meadow.

0.4 Turn left and ascend very steeply along edge of meadow with outstanding view.

0.5 Bench on left. Bear right around trees ahead.

0.6 Cross stile and enter woods on old road. Generally young forest ahead, with lots of grass and low weeds on each side. Ascend gradually.

1.3 Ahead, cross intermittent stream.

1.6 Junction with North Ridge Trail.

From Upper End

0.0 Junction with North Ridge Trail. Descend gradually ahead on old road that is rapidly greening over.

0.2 Cross intermittent stream.

0.3 Generally young forest ahead with lots of grass and low weeds on each side.

1.0 Cross stile and enter hillside meadow with outstanding view. Bear left around trees and skirt left edge of meadow.

1.1 Bench on right. Continue along edge of meadow and descend very steeply.

1.2 Turn right at foot of meadow and skirt edge.

1.3 Turn left into woods and descend on old road. Pass Snowden Manor ruins on right. Stone chimney, house foundation, and well are visible. Ahead, go left at fork off road and onto path. Pass more ruins on right and ascend past intersecting path on right.

1.4 Hillside meadow with outstanding view. A short detour reaches a bench a short distance up hill on left. To stay on Trail, stay right and descend very steeply into woods along creek.

1.5 Pass immense hickory. Go right at "T" intersection. Ahead, leave woods on gravel path at foot of meadow.

1.6 Junction with Gap Run Trail.

Piedmont Overlook Trail
Distance: 0.6 mi (*red-blazed*)

From Lower End (red-blazed). From road at west end of Visitor Center parking lot, take graveled path to left of private driveway for 0.1 mi. to reach beginning of Trail description.

0.0 At lower junction with North Ridge Trail, bear right and follow red-blazed trail as it parallels a fence. In 30 yd, bear left and follow cut path and posts up ridge-meadow.

0.4 Two benches at top of meadow, with broadest view in Park. Ahead, cross stile.

0.5 Enter woods. Descend.

0.6 Upper junction with North Ridge Trail, at 1.1 mi from *AT*.

From Upper End (red-blazed)

0.0 Junction with North Ridge Trail, at 1.1 mi from *AT*. Ascend.

0.1 Cross stile and come to two benches on hillside meadow, with broadest view in Park. Descend steeply through center of meadow, following cut path and posts.

0.5 Near bottom, pass small footpath intersecting on left. Path bears right, crosses footbridge, and then curves left toward gravel path.

0.6 Cross stile onto gravel walkway at lower junction with North Ridge Trail, 0.1 mi from Visitor Center parking lot.

SHELTERS AND CABINS

Hikers of this section of the *AT* are fortunate in having well-built and attractively located shelters that are an easy-to-moderate day's walk apart. Hikers will find that they often have the opportunity to choose their shelters according to the distance they prefer to hike.

These shelters are generally three-sided structures with raised wooden floors. Most have fireplaces and pit toilets. (Exceptions are noted in the Trail sections.) The spring at Rocky Run is seasonal.

Shelters are open to hikers for free on a first-come, first-served basis, *but early arrivals should admit latecomers up to the capacity of the shelter.* Users are expected not to deface the shelters, tables, fireplaces, etc., and they should carry out all of their trash.

Some animals in Maryland and northern Virginia, particularly raccoons, may carry rabies. Leaving behind garbage or unused food, which attracts animals, is therefore especially hazardous to the welfare of other hikers. For more information on rabies, see "Use of the Trail." Caution should be used at all times with fires, which should be confined to the fireplaces and never left untended. Fires should be out to the last spark before hikers leave the shelter.

Firewood is a problem near most of the shelters, but a little scouting through the woods generally will turn up enough dry wood. In no event are standing trees (live or dead) to be cut or defaced. Hikers also are asked to leave a small supply of dry wood inside for others, who may arrive late at night or in a storm. The courtesy will be returned.

On the following list, the distances shown are from the preceding shelter, north to south. Distances do not include the length of the shelter-access trails.

SHELTER CHART

State/ Section	Shelter	Location (mile mark)	Distance between shelters (miles)
Maryland			
1	Raven Rock	4.9/1.0	9.8
2	Ensign Phillip Cowall Memorial Shelter	3.9/0.2	8.2
5	Pine Knob	8.0/0.6	8.2
5	Rocky Run	2.0/5.4	7.5
5	Crampton Gap	7.0/0.4	5.0
6	Ed Garvey	3.7/3.0	4.1
Virginia			
2	David Lesser	3.0/10.5	12.3
2	Hikers' Cabin (Blackburn Trail Center)	6.2/7.3	3.2
3	Sam Moore	3.6/10.5	10.9
3	Rod Hollow	10.5/3.6	6.9
4	Dick's Dome	4.9/6.9	8.5
4	Manassas Gap	9.3/2.5	4.4
5	Jim and Molly Denton	3.0/5.2	5.5
6	Tom Floyd Wayside	2.9/0.7	8.1

Bear Spring Cabin and Blackburn Trail Center

Bear Spring Cabin, in Maryland Section 5, is the only cabin open to the public within the area covered by this Guide. It is a one-room, log structure on 1 acre of land donated to the PATC in 1939 by Harrison S. Krider. No more than six persons, including children, may use the cabin and surrounding area overnight. The cabin is provided with necessary equipment, including pans, dishes, cutlery, wood stove, blankets, mattresses, and bunks, but no lighting sources are available. All the user need bring is personal gear, additional bedding (usually a sleeping bag), lighting sources (flashlights or lanterns), and food. A spring and privy are nearby. For access, see Bear Spring Cabin Trail, under *"Side Trails."*

The cabin is locked. Arrangements for use, for a small fee, may be made up to eight weeks in advance by calling Cabin Reservations at PATC Headquarters (703-242-0315) between 11:30 a.m and 1:30 p.m. Mon.-Fri.

The Blackburn Trail Center (see Virginia Section 2) is available for use by PATC members, or groups, for a small fee. Reservations are required, and may be made up to two months in advance, but exclusive use of the Center is not guaranteed. Call Cabin Reservations (see previous paragraph) to make reservations and to obtain information about who will be using the Center on specific dates. The Center has a full-time caretaker from April through September, but is locked at other times. The neighboring Hodgson house has been converted into a primitive hikers'cabin that accommodates eight. It has beds and a wood stove, but no mattresses or other equipment. It is open all year and is free to *AT* thru-hikers.

INDEX

G

H

I

J

PATC INFORMATION

Web: www.patc.net

Phone: 703-242-0315

Staff Office hours: Regular business hours

Cabin and Customer Service Desks hours:
Monday to Friday, 11:30 a.m.–1:30 p.m.

Fax: 703-242-0968 (available 24 hours/day)

Address: 118 Park Street, SE, Vienna, VA 22180-4609